Several Encounters of the Supernatural

SEVERAL ENCOUNTERS OF THE SUPERNATURAL

A true story of A Young Woman's Battle with

Demonic Forces and How She Won the Victory

Tyniesha Walker

XULON PRESS

Xulon Press
2301 Lucien Way #415
Maitland, FL 32751
407.339.4217
www.xulonpress.com

© 2020 by Tyniesha Walker

All rights reserved solely by the author. The author guarantees all contents are original and do not infringe upon the legal rights of any other person or work. No part of this book may be reproduced in any form without the permission of the author. The views expressed in this book are not necessarily those of the publisher.

Printed in the United States of America.

ISBN-13: 978-1-6305-0387-1

Table of Contents

Ch. 1: Meeting the Wolf in Sheep's Clothing 1

Ch. 2: Beginning of The Fall 7

Ch. 3: Deception of A Satanic Lover 17

Ch. 4: Cursed with A Blessed Pregnancy 23

Ch. 5: Consumed by Demons with A 2nd Pregnancy 33

Ch. 6: The Power of Demonized Territory 41

Ch. 7: Redemption by a miracle 47

Ch. 8: Roots from the beginning: A Shocking Revelation sent from heaven 57

Ch. 9: A 2nd Affliction: A different kind of testimony 61

God's Glory. 79

My name is Tyniesha I was born in Long Island, NY on November 29, 1984. I have three siblings a sister and two brothers. I have always been a humble body person, and always have been peculiar. I moved to Pensacola, FL with my mom and brother when I was five years old. I lived with my mom for a short amount of years because my mom had another baby which was my sister.

I went to live with my great aunt at the age of eight years old. My mom then had my sister, and oldest brother to attend to. That's when I stayed at my aunt's house to go to school. I was in elementary at the time. I was a second grader and I was an honor roll student always quiet, and was admirable of reading. I was pretty healthy for the most part although I was said to have always had an issue with the common sickness constipation. I had that problem since my birth.

I didn't have my father in my life, but I always had a desire for him to be there. While I was staying with my aunt I was introduced to going to church. She was my second mother and always treated me as such. She was an older woman and was born in the country. She was elderly age, but she still had a strong spiritual background so she kept me grounded.

I was forced to go to church every time the doors were opened. I didn't understand the purpose in it. So, I was traditionally attending. I got baptized at eleven years old, and joined the choir. I took summer trips with my church and attended other events. I stayed with my aunt until I was thirteen years old, and finally was granted permission to move back with my mom.

Several Encounters of the Supernatural

I was so happy and excited to go back to my family. My mom had another baby at the time whom was my youngest brother. As I moved back with my mom. I stopped attending church. I was in middle school by that time. It was eighth grade then and I was still doing really well in school. I had a few friends. I wasn't the popular one and didn't desire to be. When I turned fifteen years old. I started changing and went through a very isolative stage in my life.

I secluded myself from everyone and just started staying in the house all summer long. I didn't go anywhere at all. I stayed in my room and didn't do anything. It was supposed to be a temporary stage, but it took over me and instead of short term it turned out long term. I wanted to come out, but couldn't. I started feeling very lonely on the inside.

How much I desired my dad, but couldn't have him. It started one night my first encounter with the spiritual realm. I felt something all around me, but didn't know what it was. I had an eerie feeling something was taunting me and this occurrence was only at night. I found myself waking up every night to this situation. I even started feeling as if my heart was going into overdrive, and it was starting to give me chest pains.

I thought I was having heart palpitations and felt very sick. I would wake up every night at 1am and wake my mom up to tell her something was wrong. She was getting upset because I would wake her up from her sleep. She would say, "Dog Tyniesha!" You waking me up from my sleep I don't see anything!" Then she would put on gospel music. It was only getting worse not better, and so my mom decided to take me to the hospital.

I waited in the ER to get exams and the doctor ruled didn't see anything wrong. Everything was normal and then he asked. "Are you worried about anything?" I responded, "Yes!" "The world coming to an end!" He looked at me and said, "this could be anxiety taking over you." He left out and came back with a Christian based Psychiatrist card and said. "Give them a call." I felt foolish, and crazy for why these thoughts even taunted me like they did.

It even started affecting my day at school because this aura was following me everywhere. I was being consumed mentally and spiritually. One day I had it in my spirit to go back to church, and I did. I became a faithful walker in the word of God. I was very young, and didn't understand much about it. I started going every time the doors were opened, and I actually go in attentive in what was being said.

I always enjoyed being there. I found it to be comforting and soothing for my soul. It also stopped that strange aura from following me! I finally felt peace and was able to sleep again. I was the only one in my family that enjoyed it that much and attended regularly. I desired for my other family members to go, but they didn't find it to be for them. .

I desired for everyone to live according to his word, but they didn't. I was told to continue going because they were coming in, but they never did. So, I stopped attending because I had no support in it. I had turned my back on God. My life took a left dark turn after I made that decision. The following were chapters that occurred in my life in my early twenties.

They were rare and unusual. They were unexplainable. There were also very harsh times of turmoil for me. Chapter one is about someone that entered into my family circle that couldn't be trusted. Chapter two is about the very first occurrence of me literally breaking down and entering a season of sickness like never before that took everything from me, and literally tried to claim my life.

Chapter three is about me befriending someone from a dark world, and the consequences that came after. The rest of the chapters are in order as they actually happened. I never saw myself as writing a book. When other people heard of my story. They suggested I could write a book about what I had experienced. I didn't consider it until I heard from God. He ordered me to share my story with the world. I didn't know where to start as far as structure.

God literally gave me the title of every chapter I had to endure. He then started speaking to me to put the story in his order. People always respond with a reaction of shock when I tell them what I went through. Some don't believe my story. Some say "How did you survive all of that?" Some understand that it wasn't me. My life has purpose and God is in full control. Now I gladly share my story because I want people to know that nothing is impossible for God to handle. This is my true life story and how it began.

CH.1

Meeting the Wolf in Sheep's Clothing

This began when I was twenty-one years old. The year was 2006. I was working at a convenience store. I was living in my own place alone. My mom stayed down the road about a mile away. I was always real close to my mom. We had a positive and close relationship. I was at her place often. My mom was single at the time.

She had a female friend whom she hanged with very often. Her friend wasn't single. She had a boyfriend. The boyfriend had a male friend whom he introduced to my mom. The guy's name was Jumbo Bones. My mom met the guy and was swept off her feet at first sight. Jumbo was a 5'7" dark skinned figure. He weighed about one hundred sixty-five lbs. He was well dressed, and wore slacks with nice collar shirts and dress shoes.

He also wore a du rag with colorful rubber bands tied down the back of the du rag. It seemed as a great relationship for about three months or so. One day I was at my mom's house with my siblings. My mom was on a date with Jumbo. She came home later that evening, and I overheard Jumbo calling her out her name. After that incident It became habitual.

He would talk to her in disrespectful ways. I was fed up! I didn't want to see her self-esteem attacked in that manner. This man had a very dark side that had been revealed to me. I went to my mom to warn her about this guy. He was affecting her self-esteem. He was verbally abusing her. I informed her about his dark side. She defended him. She responded, "I need him!" I responded. "You don't need him!" "You can do bad by yourself!"

I couldn't fathom the way he treated her! My mom had been blinded by this guy. She didn't understand how detrimentally exhausting her spirit had become. It had been six months into the relationship. Around late Sept 2006 he informed her of some furniture he was giving away. My mom asked me to assist her with moving it. As we arrived, we saw a great amount of furniture in the garage.

I recognized a nice table and asked, "How much do you want for it?" He said, "$25.00 and its yours!" "Okay." I responded. When we were moving the chair, which was brown in color and wooden. I walked over a stomp that was connected to a small tree. As I was walking, I felt an eerie sensation, like warm air came upon me. I thought for a second. Then brushed it off.

About a week after the incident. I started feeling depressed, and lonely. I didn't understand what was going on with me. I even stopped feeling like myself. I found myself crying many times about nothing. I felt a negative force following me. I was at work one day and started feeling very sick. I felt very unusual with pressure on the left side of my temple. It felt as if someone had placed a hammer at the corner of my eye and just left it there!

! I never felt anything like it before. It wasn't a migraine. It was like someone was squeezing my temple, and pressing into the corner of my eye. My first thought was to treat as a headache and take aspirin. My stomach also was feeling uneasy. I brushed it off as if it were a 24 hour virus. I continue to work at the convenient store until md November 2006.

Meeting The Wolf In Sheep's Clothing

I quit because of miss abuse of employment. I still had my own place and continued to pay bills with money I had saved up for rainy days. I was in between jobs and looking for work in other places, but no luck. Jumbo Bones was beginning to be a lot nicer to me. He even asked me to help assist in making flyers for his new business. I finally started seeing him in a different way.

Maybe the guy I wasn't so fond about wasn't so bad after all. Maybe he has changed. I started speaking with him more. He even invited me over to his house for gatherings, and events. I started opening up to him. One day I was at his house. It was just me and him. I was helping him on the internet with business cards. He asked. "Do you think I should go get your mom now or later?" I responded, "It's totally up to you!" He said, "I'm going to take a break from work, and go get us some Chinese Food to eat."

He left to go get the food. When he returned. We ate some lunch and talked. Then he decided to go get my mom. I stayed at his house, and waited for him to return. He came back with my mom, sister, and her friend. I greeted them when they came together and no one spoke. I asked "What's wrong?" Mom said, "Be quiet and don't say anything!" I responded, "why can't I talk?" what you mean?" Then Jumbo blurted out "Shut up I don't want to hear any talking!"

I grew confused as to how one minute he was nice, and friendly. The next minute he turned into a hateful maniac. My thoughts were a dark cloud has come upon him and no one could explain it. Later on, that night while in the den at his place while watching television. I heard him talking to someone, but everyone was in the other side of the house. He was in the kitchen which was next to the den. I asked him. "Did you say something?" but he didn't respond.

He startled me because he was just standing there with a dark demonic look in his eyes. Then he just walked away. I was puzzled about this man's behavior. I told my mom something was seriously wrong here. She agreed this time but she just shook it off again.

As time was going by my mom was getting aggravated with her situation.

However, he was trying to buy her love back. He promised he wouldn't do it anymore. He decided to throw her a surprise birthday party in summer of August 2007. She accepted the invitation. He invited everyone to his house. He cooked cheese rolls, rotel dip, and cake. The cake was very odd looking. It had my mom picture in the middle. Baby, Nephew, Aunt, Cousin, Mother, and Sister written all over the cake.

It didn't have Happy Birthday anywhere on it. We just laughed, and said. What the heck? My mom said Jumbo always doing something crazy like that! Then I started to think maybe he just different. The arguments grew with my mom and Jumbo. He continued to say he was sorry and don't pay him any attention! He started taking me back and forth to work for the price of $50.00 every two weeks.

I started being nice to him for the sake of my mom. I was working at the hotel. I was a front desk clerk. One day while checking in customers, and sitting at the desk. Jumbo showed up at my job unannounced. When he arrives. He presented a box of chicken with an orange soda. I was so adored to see him bring me something to eat when I least expected it. I was highly grateful, and he told me, "I thought you would like something to eat." "Your welcome!" Just then he won me over.

I befriended him and was cordial to him. He made a second trip to my job unannounced. It was a Sunday afternoon. This time he had a plate that he prepared himself. Once again, I was impressed and grateful. Then he said, "I'm about to take your mom a plate now." "This the Sunday dinner I made for you all." The plate was very tempting. It had broiled chicken, cornbread, potatoes, and cabbage. I ate every bit of it. Then I called my mom while at work and told her Jumbo had just brought me a plate of food and had she eaten her food yet? She said she hadn't received a plate, and she hadn't seen him. I told her "He said he had fix Sunday dinner for us." She said, "He didn't tell me anything about it." I just brushed it off. I said, "Well I got one and I ate it!"

CH. 2

Beginning of The Fall

---✝---

It was one day me and my mom was talking. She was explaining how she was tired and fed up. She was definitely ready to move on, and if God just made a way for her to walk then she wouldn't return. She told me that she was breaking up with Jumbo. She said, "It's a wrap!" It was February 8, 2008. The night after I had an outer body experience. I lifted up my eyes in a very dark deep pit like dungeon with flames of fire the height of mountains all around me.

I was on a white stretcher, and it protected me. I was safe as long as I stayed on the stretcher. My arm fell off the stretcher, and the fire burned my wrist. I woke up I could still feel the burning sensation in my wrist! I started to feel uncertain around the morning hours, but I wasn't sure of what was going on. It was exactly one week later while I was at work. I started feeling a burning bubbly feeling in my stomach.

I thought I had to go to the bathroom. When I went to the restroom there was nothing to come. My stomach felt like a volcano wanting to erupt, but no justice. I was working front desk around this time. It was about six o' clock in the evening. It was dark outside. I was sitting at the desk trying to bear the pain. Thinking it was going to pass over. It got so bad I asked my manager to leave, and he saw the agony I was in, and allowed me to take the rest of the day off. I called my aunt to come get me, and informed her of the situation.

My aunty said she'll be there soon. When my aunt picked me up. She saw what I was going through and became overwhelmed with sadness. She asked me. "What was wrong?" "How did I get like this?" "Did I want to go to the hospital?" I told her I don't know but I was crying hysterically. She took me to my mom's house when I went inside my mom ask me" "What was wrong?" "How was I feeling?" I told her bad! She then asked, "What happened?" I told her I didn't know. She said she would cook something to eat.

She made fried chicken, cabbage, and cornbread. I started to eat the cabbage when I swallowed the cabbage. I had a very uncomfortable rumbling in my stomach and the food came back up very slimy from my mouth. My mom was in a panic. Oh my gosh what is going on with you? I couldn't eat or drink for three days straight, and then it just stopped by itself. I returned back to work as normal. I was fine for about a week. The sickness started again while at work. I asked my manager once again. "Can I go home?" He allowed me.

My aunty was called once again. She came and picked me up. Took me to my mom's house. My mom was very puzzled by this time as to what was going on. She said," "Your sick again?" "How do you keep getting like this?" I responded, "I don't know!" She responded. "Aww man." She was starting to become worried. I was twenty-three years old at this time.

I started losing weight without notice. I wasn't able to eat. Every time I tried to take some food in. I would feel so sick. I was getting dehydrated. My mom suggested I go to the hospital. I decided to go because the pain was unbearable. I felt something was hovering over me like a warm sensation. My eyes were rolling and I was so weak I couldn't stand up. The doctor gave me a strong dose of pain medicine and immediately my mind start easing and my body went numb. The doctor did an X-ray and lab work. He said I had the stomach flu. I felt at ease thinking it's nothing major. The doctor sent me home with medicine, and told me to rest. He suggested I drink clear fluids only.

I went back to my mom's house and gave her the doctors report. She felt relieved to know it was temporary sickness. A few days went by and things started getting worse. Someone suggested we go to another doctor, and so we did. This doctor was very concerned when she looked at me. She also took tests, x-rays, and even an AIDS test.

There was rapid weight loss. She was telling me. I look too frail. She knew something was going on. She was determined to find the underlying issue. I told her the previous doctor diagnosed stomach flu. She said. "You don't have the stomach flu!" When tests came back everything was negative. They sent me home with phenergan and other stomach meds.

I didn't make it back to work. This sickness started consuming me on a daily basis. I would try to eat and my stomach would become like a boiling pot of grits with my organs twisting. My weight started at 105 pounds 5'3" tall. I was always petite, but never this frail. I became gaunt and started looking like a skeleton frame. I couldn't drink water. It would just come back up like a gushing water geyser. The meds they gave me wasn't helping. I started questioning myself. Like, what was really going on?

The doctors are saying nothing is wrong! One doctor even said, "She is too frail, and needs to eat something fast before she dies." My mom asked, "What can she eat?" The doctor responded, "Anything!" "Just feed her." My mom said, "But nothing stays down!" and the doctor insisted nothing was wrong I was just anorexic. I was down to 80 pounds by this time. Doctors were just sending me out the door. My aunt became involved, and started calling different places for help. She told a good friend about my situation.

Several Encounters of the Supernatural

The friend knew a doctor out of town in Panama City, Florida that was willing to help. She made arrangements with my mom for me to be seen. When I arrived at the doctors' office. She did the usual procedure. Then looked at my labs, and made arrangements for me to get hospitalized. That night around 10 pm I was placed in the hospital. My mom stayed with me so I wouldn't be left alone. They placed me in a bed. Then hooked me up to the IV, and gave me demerol. I was at ease for a moment, and then I was gasping faintly like I was losing breath. I couldn't talk at all.

My eyes were bulked like a bull frog, and my mom asked. "What's wrong?" She then called the nurse in. She saw the state I was in, and attempted to calm me down. Once everything was peaceful. She said, I had an anxiety attack, and that it was an effect from the demerol. The next day they had an upper endoscopy scheduled. That is when they place a scope in the upper G.I tract to see what's going on. The only thing it read was a swollen esophagus.

The following day they scheduled a colonoscopy. That is when you drink a gallon of go lightly substance to clean the colon, and check for polyps and cancerous tissue. When the test results came back it was normal. They continued with fluids, and had me on solids. The whole time I was there I was fine no symptoms occurred. I was there for 5 days, and then released. It wasn't even 48 hours later before the symptoms started again.

I returned home back to Pensacola, FL. I woke up. with no strength, and my health had deteriorated dramatically. I had a younger brother who was fifteen years-old at the time. He saw the condition I was in. He humbled himself, and allowed me to rest on him. Then later that evening my mom was playing gospel music. It was an album Jumbo had left for her in the mailbox. She had a few friends over, and they decided to read the bible.

Next thing I remember I fell over my stomach, and started screaming at the top of my lungs. My mom described those events as follows. She was going to call the ambulance, and I immediately got off my brother. I then behaved as if nothing was wrong. She says. I told her. "I didn't want to go to the hospital." "I'm just fine." There is nothing wrong. I ran swiftly to the back of her room. She said, "What do you mean there's nothing wrong!" She looked at me with a very peculiar expression on her face.

I then got off her bed, and went back to the living room. Everyone was sitting in there. She continued. She said. I sat straight up on the sofa at her place. I looked across the room at her, and my sister. She says. I gave them a look so fierce, and didn't crack a smile on my face. My eyes turned bloodshot red, and they were becoming frightened by the image they saw. My mom then goes on to say. I stood straight up looked at my fifteen year- old brother. I pointed at him, and spoke, "I'M GOING TO KILL YOU!" Then she says I fell to my knees, and started sobbing speaking, help me! help me! help me please! My mom was very confused as to what was going on.

My mom says. She called the ambulance because I just started screaming to the top of my lungs. It was 20 minutes later when they arrived at my mom's house. She says. I perked up out of the blue. I said, "I'm fine!" She responded, "Are you sure?" "what's going on?" You've been laying down whining, being helpless, and now you say, "Your fine!" "What's really going on with you?" I said, "nothing I'm fine." Then she said. When the ambulance left.

I returned to my previous condition. I was whining, crying, and asking someone to help because it hurts! My mom was pained by what she was seeing. She started losing hope. She couldn't see around our situation. My mom reached out to a dear friend. She knew they had a close relationship with God. She invited the woman over to see if she could help. The woman came over one evening while I was laying on the couch.

She put her hand on me, and began to pray in silence. When she finished. She told my mom that Satan had a stronghold on my organs! However, we didn't really understand what that meant at the time. I remember telling my mom," I needed a witch doctor!" My mom asked, "What is that?" I responded, "I don't know!" I didn't understand why I was saying this. Many strange events took place during that time.

I had to quit my job, and leave my place of residence. I had to go back under my mom's care. I got hospitalized again at a nearby hospital for a month straight. They gave me a catheter so they could feed me nutrition. It was so bad they were feeding me through a peg tube. They had inserted into my stomach. As soon as they would push it in with a syringe it be regurgitating through my mouth all at once. Then they would feed me through a catheter. It was inserted through the vein of my arm.

It was giving me nutrition but wasn't putting any weight on me at all. It couldn't be used long term, or would cause serious infection that could claim my life. After the doctors done all they felt was necessary. I was released once again into the world. I go back home, and go right back to bed. I became dependent in every area of my life. I was twenty-four years-old at this time. My mom had to bathe, clothe, and feed me through the tube. It was just hopeless. One night I was feeling such strong forces. They were making me feel weak, fatigue, and just drilling in my back. As if someone was beating me in it with a hot pole. I told my mom to just end it for me. Please take me out of my misery. She said sadly sobbing, "I can't do that!" "I said please, "I can't take this anymore just end it!" My mom said, "Stop talking like that!" I said sobbing sadly, "You don't know what it feels like!" You're not the one going through it!"

Please! Just then an old family member came in. He saw my agony. He put his head down, and started praying before me. Everyone around me was well, and happy. They were living their life. They were going to the movies, parties, and out to eat. They were attending school. I mean just enjoying life. There I was tied to a bed, and couldn't do anything! I cried and felt tortured.

The sickness had a pattern to it. I would be down for three straight days, and up the next two days. Then I would go right back down, and it was like this for two years straight. I was up long enough to get a little energy. I would go right back to torture, and heat. I had got down to 73 pounds by this time. I looked like a total skeletal frame. My face had become half of what it was normally.

My lips swelled up bigger than my face. My eyes became big, and bulked. My chest had become a bone, and my chest area were completely gone! The fat had been consumed. My stomach became sunk in, and you could see my rib cage bone. My legs were just a bone. No muscle was present. I couldn't stand up on my own. My collarbone was protruded all the way out.

My feet had taken a turn, and were twisted like a dog's feet. My fingernails had grown like vampire nails. My hair had grown out really long pass my back. My backside which normally was curved outward. My tailbone was now visible. My c-spine bone was showing in clarity. You could see the imprint of every one of them. My tailbone was showing. All the flesh on it had completely vanished.

People who knew me heard about what I was going through. They wanted to get a glimpse of me. However, the minute they saw me. They couldn't stand to look at me. It hurt them to see me in that condition. It was September of 2009. My mom had got in touch with another friend. This friend also knew someone that was close to God. He made arrangements to come to my house to pray for me.

They showed up, and walked into my room. When the other guy saw me. He was amazed, and baffled at what he saw. He says. It was so bad he thought, "I had AIDS!" He went on to pray for me, and even encouraged me to try to lift my spirit. He started coming over every night to check on me. He read the word of God for encouragement. He even would take me to doctor appointments, and try to encourage me. He was showing me how to fight back what I was dealing with.

I started to feel uplifted in spirit. I also believed that he was an angel sent by God. Before this time, no one showed so much support other than my mom. I didn't know a stranger could care so much about someone he didn't know. One night he was expected to come by. My mom said he was running a little late. He asked her to hold on a little longer, and he was still coming.

My mom explains of another strange event that goes as follows. She says. She was sitting on her recliner chair. She was rocking, and I was laying on the floor next to a pail of vomit. She says. I was laying there with my eyes closed. She says. She called my name, and told me to come to her. Then she says. I got up like on all four limbs. In the manner of a dog, and started to come toward her. I then stopped in the middle of the floor, and just looked at her. I went back to laying down next to the pail of vomit. An hour after the guy came over. He took me in the room, and was holding me like a little baby. He was rocking me, and praying over me as I was crying help me. He explained some strange events as well.

They go as follows. I stopped crying. Then I started scratching my fingernails across my face. I then started laughing out of nowhere. Then he said. I stood up, and just started howling from my soul. After that night he ruled out that this was demonic possession, and he was going to get his pastor to do an exorcism. The pastor came a week later. It went as follows. He came early at dawn.

He asked the spirit, "Who are you?" and "What are you doing here?" He then used an anointed cross to draw the demon out. All I remember is when the cross touched me. I Felt a lot of heat around me, and started howling from my soul! I felt a force of heat released. I went fast asleep afterwards, and didn't wake up until hours later. When I got up. I felt like a brand-new person, and finally at peace. I hadn't felt that in the past two years. He then said. The lord instructed him to tell me to eat nectar from fruits for the next seven days.

I was obedient. It was gone!! I received my breakthrough! So, I started healing spiritually, and physically. I was reading my word The New Testament. I was going to church, and giving God glory. He brought me out and delivered me. I was talking to Barracuda who was imprisoned at that time. He was rejoicing because he was able to hear my voice again.

I wasn't dead but alive and well. We made arrangements so that we could see each other. I was happy! I could enjoy life again after two years of torture and torment. Me, and my mom went to visit him on Mother's Day. It was on a Sunday May 2010. I enjoyed the visitation. However, I felt terror on every side, and even felt a dark force with me. It took my appetite away when I was there, but when I left. I would get really hungry. I didn't understand this concept. While I would visit the prison. I couldn't eat anything, and felt very unusual. When I would leave those grounds. I felt normal again.

I would feel fine! This happened every time I would go. After my deliverance from these demons. I felt a void left with me, and I felt like the loneliest person I know. All I endured for so long, I still didn't understand, and I still didn't know my purpose. One night I felt a strong twisting in my intestines, and I went to the restroom.

I thought I had to go, but instead there was nothing. The pain just continued. I finally came out of the restroom because something was just holding my intestines, and it literally felt like they were on fire with bubbles. As I sat outside the bathroom door I started screaming again to the top of my lungs. My mom had come to see what was wrong and she said, "TYNIESHA!" She said. I started laughing and then I slapped her.

She got on the phone, and was telling someone it had come back!! This time it was causing me to throw up a green substance, and I hadn't eaten anything green. Then I started throwing up a brown substance. I would throw up for three-four days straight. I couldn't take in water, broth, ensure, soups, crackers, grits, or candy. Nothing would stay down at all. Other times my stomach would twist up in knots so bad. I would drink something, and one second later it would all come back up. I stayed in bed with a mop bucket next to my bedside full of vomit. It became my lifestyle.

My mom took me to the hospital. They hospitalized me for a few days because by this time it became known to them for me to be dehydrated. I would always have extremely low levels of potassium and calcium. While I was there my mom explains of another strange event that occurred. It went as follows. I was laying in the hospital bed, and a cloud of dark smoke in the form of a demon face raised up from my stomach area. As it raised up my eyes got big, and bulk. As it proceeded to exit the hospital room my eyes went back to normal. My mom couldn't believe what she saw, but knew what she saw.

CH. 3

Deception of A Satanic Lover

---- ✝ ----

It was ongoing for some time and I even started dreaming of evil all around me. It was early in the summer of June 2010. My mom was trying to find a solution to this problem. She continued her search to save me in any way she could. She found one of her ex's cousin, and went to her hairstylist to get her hair done. While there she explained the situation that we were having.

This person told her of another friend that had a similar situation, and knew of someone that could help. My mom was grateful, and immediately took the friend's number down to call. She spoke with her of a woman she knew that could have had the solution. She couldn't give out personal information. So, she would drive to go pick up the woman, and bring her back.

The woman was tall and bright-skinned with eyeliner that extended out the corner of her eyes. She introduced herself as Mrs. Acosta Deez. She was very soft spoken and a beautiful smile. She entered into my room, and sat on my bed. She looked at me. I was relieved to see her come to my aid. She didn't hesitate to say she was a psychic vampire. I didn't know what that was. She then went to tell me things that she couldn't of possibly have known because I have never seen her before in my life.

She informed that doctors said I was anorexic,, but she didn't see that ever being in my life. She also said people in my past believed I buy my friends. However, they were wrong because I just did things for people to show them that I care. I was ready to run out of my bed because she scared me with that information. She was so keen on point. I asked her. "Could she help me?"

I whispered with pity and sorrow in my voice. She went on to say yes. She will help me, and would be my nurse for the week. She said, "What is the date?" Then she responded the June 4. She said give me until the July 4 and you'll receive your healing. I was so ecstatic. All my faith went into her words. I just felt I had been tortured so long. I wanted anything to make them go away. Meanwhile, she told us that I was possessed with demons. She said they had full control.

She said they came from someone that fed me potatoes, and that's how they manifested in my stomach. She said. I had been like this for two and a half years. She asked to see a picture because I stepped over something that wasn't originally meant for me. We showed her a picture, and she said. He despised women, and he is demon possessed.

This was the ex. Whom name is Jumbo. She went on to say. He did this on purpose. He wanted my mom to himself, and he was planning to extinguish me out the picture. Of all her children, I was considered the weakest link. That's why I was attacked first. She also included he placed a generational curse on the whole family. That was the purpose of the cake.

She didn't leave out the fact that the reason for all of this was because my mom broke up with him. He had bitter love. She gave us a lot of insight about the spiritual realm, and a lot of knowledge as well. We took heed to, but at the same time. I fell victim to what we were told. I let my guard down completely because I felt compassion for her.

She told us about a scripture in the bible that talks about giving Jesus frankincense and myrrh. They are herbs and that's what they used to heal. She gave me very specific instructions on what to do and when to do it. She informed us that she didn't do bad things just the good side. I believed her because just as she promised I really received my healing on the date she said I would.

I was able to eat again. In fact, my appetite increased in double size, and of course I was happy. I had a lot to make up for. I started shopping, and going out to eat. We became best friends, and I loved her. I believed anything she said. There was a spiritual connection between us. I loved being around her. She was so much fun.

How she could see through people lives. I desired to have her gift because It was like nothing I ever knew. She understood what I had been going through, and she made my problem go away. So, I started glorifying her of course. When I asked her. How did she do it? She said it's not her, but God, and if she didn't give him the credit. He would take the power she had away.

I said, "Ok", but I really had become wrapped up in her way of life. I Started seeing the spiritual realm in a different way. I never knew anything about getting entangled in the universe until she came along. The things we were involved in were of witchcraft, and not of God. Someone warned me. You're not supposed to do that! I was not hearing them because all I saw was salvation when it came to her. Every time someone said something about her.

I defended her honor. I felt she was the god, and the gospel. Satan had deceived me horribly. My doings went completely against God's word which says Don't have any other gods before me. (Exodus20:2) Don't deal in sorcery, witchcraft, necromancers, and familiar spirits. Have nothing to do with those things at all (Leviticus 20:6) However, at this time we were doing all of the above. I became so blinded with the seeds we were planting.

I actually believed that nothing was wrong, and everything was of God. I had been deceived greatly! Me and Barracuda who was imprisoned. We discussed us starting a family when he came home. I had no children at the time. I was heartbroken because I didn't want to die without my bloodline thriving. I was the last of my dad's side. The generation was deceased.

I desired to have a child. Sadly, I never got to see my birth dad again. I believed if he was with me. Then I wouldn't have went through it. He would've protected me. When I found out there wouldn't be any more searching for him on the earth. He was demised. This caused a bad seed to generate in my heart. It was almost as I was accepting death.

If I could only continue my bloodline. I was twenty-five at this time. I had gained a good amount of weight, and I was gaining it before I knew it. Everything was filling back out my spinal cord was covered again. My legs, arms, collarbone, and ribcage were all covered with flesh again. I had gained forty-two pounds in a five-month span. I just knew I was on my way. Woohoo! Thank you, God! Credit goes to Mrs. Acosta, right? Wrong! I was placed under a healing curse. Not a real healing, but another spell on top of a spell.

This meant even more problems. You see Satan can't drive out Satan. God's word tells us Satan can't drive out Satan because then he will be divided against himself and therefore how will his kingdom stand? (Luke 11:15) In other words I wasn't helping myself. I was hurting myself and, this was disobedience. Satan doesn't want to drive out Satan because then his kingdom would be torn down. So, how was I expecting to get delivered by Satan. Satan was the one who had the stronghold on me! Time was going forward, and I had so much I needed to do, yet I wasn't doing much with myself.

We had moved from our current residence, and I was getting caught up in my past. I was forgetting who I was, and what my goals were supposed to be. My mind got caught up in the very wrong things. I had a knew belief system one that God wasn't happy about. I even stopped believing in the name of Jesus. I was led astray in the wilderness. Although I believed I was on my way to redemption. Moving forward she went her way, and I went mine. What lied ahead was much more deadly.

Ch. 4

Cursed with A Blessed Pregnancy

The date was January 1, 2011. Barracuda was released from prison. We met up of course, and I had a strange spiritual aura that was with me in his presence. I didn't understand it, but it was not good! It's as if something wasn't following me, but literally on me. He kept his part of the bargain about us starting a family so my bloodline could survive. After he left me.

I felt very sick and depressed. I was walking outside my residence because I needed fresh air. I couldn't eat a thing all over again. A voice came to me while walking, and said you are pregnant. I was like "Huh," "No I'm not!" "Can't be!" I actually was sick, and when he came around. He had expressed that he believed I had conceived. I was in denial I didn't believe it.

He suggested I take a test to find out. I did as I was asked, and read my results. They were indeed positive, and I was so overjoyed about my little one! I was scared too! I didn't know how to take the fact that someone was going to be kicking in my belly, and I wasn't going to be able to stop it. However, that desire for my bloodline to survive had been met. I was glowing. I even had a baby bump at two months.

Everyone knew it was what I wanted, and they were all so happy! They knew of all I had been through. They felt I deserved it. I was so excited! Who will he or she look like? What will be the name? How will all of this go? Me becoming a mommy! "Awesome." "WOW!" I went to the beach one day in April while I was pregnant. I was right at three months, and everything appeared smooth at first. I really enjoyed my time at the beach.

I was really enjoying the food, and the water. Something I couldn't get away from. I was seeing Barracuda on every man's face. It was nerve wrecking, and unexplainable. Especially, since I carried alone. Barracuda decided to depart from me. However, it was the last enjoyable thing I experienced during the pregnancy. It went downhill the very next day. I woke up with a tingling aura in my fingers that extended from my intestines.

I thought I was getting a stomach virus. It wasn't even close to it. I felt excruciating burning pains from my stomach to my legs. I contacted Barracuda the following afternoon and told him something is very wrong with me. I can't tolerate anything. He said. "Ok what do you think you can eat?" I responded, "I'll try watermelon, crackers, and water." Later, on that night around eleven pm.

Barracuda arrived with the items. He came into the room, and tried to comfort me first. Then he started asking me questions. "How long you been like this?" "What's going on with you?" I responded, "I don't know!" I just know I feel horrible. He then broke a piece of watermelon, and began feeding it to me. I tried to eat it, but as soon as I attempted to swallow it.

It came gushing back up. He said, "Oh whoa!" I fed you too much at a time. I was just whining, and continuing to throw up. He was so amazed, and puzzled with what he was seeing. So, he just laid down. I laid down beside him. I was curled up. I was feeling so bad with a disgusting taste in my mouth. I had a warm tingling aura all around me. My stomach was doing flips, and every time he came near.

My energy was getting worse. I told him please no. He said he'll stay a little longer to see if I'm going to start feeling better.

About three hours later. He said. He has to go, and if I'm not feeling better. Just go to the hospital. He will meet me up there from work. I didn't want to be left alone but I had to endure it. That morning at dawn. I called the ambulance to go to the hospital. I arrived there, and they took tests.

They gave me IV fluids and Barracuda ask me about my situation. I told him I was feeling a little better. He took me to get a salad. He thought. If I had something lite to eat. Maybe I wouldn't be so bad off. He took me to my sister's house, and told me to take care of myself. He departed from me. Later that evening, I decided to eat the salad.

As soon as I started eating it. My stomach started turning, and I was throwing up again. It continued all night long. I started having nightmares of Mrs. Acosta. In one of the visions. She was standing in a very dark gloomy hallway with only candles lit. She was hexing me. In another vision. She was calling my name. It was like this all week long. That Friday morning at dawn. I told my mom something was going terribly wrong. I told her.

I needed Mrs. Acosta. She said she didn't know how to get in touch with her, or her whereabouts. I told her. I was in mega pain, and I didn't feel right. We all gathered in the car on a hunt to find her, and we located her. I approached the residence where she was, and went inside. She was sitting on a long floral chair with hot pink imprints. I immediately went to her humbly, and bow before her. I asked her what was wrong with me. She told me.

She no longer works for the good, but has made Satan her Father, and turned over to the dark side. I was so confused three months earlier she was good, and now she has gone completely black. I told her I believe. She had done something to me. She said she hadn't done anything. This has come upon you another way. She then asked me. "Where all had I been?" and "What had I done?" I told her. She decided to help me again. She said, "He wants you to give him the child!" No way this is my first child! I'm not sacrificing my child. She said, "He wants you to serve him."." "I said no." "I don't want to serve him." Then she says. "He will spare you for your child." I said, "No!" "I'm not giving up my child!"

She kept trying to convince me of this. I kept sticking to my word. She then said. "He is going to take you then." She left out, and said she had to talk to a certain spirit and see if they would help. She came back after contacting this spirit, and said, "He has control to both sides and he will see to it that your baby is ok!" Earlier that day.

Her and my mom were speaking amongst each other. She asked. My mom about informing Barracuda about sitting with me. They didn't want to leave me unattended. I said, "No!" "I don't want him here, or anywhere around me." She asked. "Why?" "When he needs to be a part of this!" I just said, "I don't want him to see me like this." She then said, "But, Tyniesha if he really loves you this wouldn't push him away." It would bring him closer."

I wasn't trying to hear what she was saying. I really didn't want him in my presence! I hated the way I felt around him. The attack would just be even worse. They contacted him anyways, and sent him over there. They went completely over my wishes. When he walked into the room. He was very angry with me for reasons of us departing. That spirit was with him. He glanced at me, and then just started staring. He approached me sat on the sofa, and started holding me. Then he started comforting me saying its ok its ok.

He had done let his guard down because of the state he saw me in. He felt sorrowful, and grief. They left him there to attend to me. He was speaking to me, but I couldn't respond I was just listening. I also couldn't look at him because the forces that was controlling me wouldn't allow me to. He was overviewing my body.

He lifted up my shirt. Observing the flesh that had been consumed from me, and he overlooked my legs. He must have seen the demon through my stomach because then he started speaking to it directly. He then placed his hand over my belly, and started praying in silence. He grew angry with me again because of the jeopardy he felt I was putting myself in, and the unborn child.

He didn't agree with me having Mrs. Acosta around because he knew what she was about. He was hesitant about being in her presence. They returned, and he departed once again. She was smart in the way she operated. She even convinced me to contact this spirit in which I did! Big mistake that was. When I got back home. I asked why do I feel like an evil force is with me. She said you're going through a spiritual change.

You're going to be ok. Later that night she stayed with me so she can watch over me. I overheard her talking to Satan. She asked him would he spare me, and take the curse off. His response was NO! because I wasn't his. She said, "I know she is not yours, but she is my friend." "Can you do it since I'm your child?" We did more work that was supposedly going to get it off. Nothing was calming this down. My mom had talk to nearby people, and informed them I was going through it again, and her work wasn't helping this time.

Meanwhile, I wasn't able to eat anything, and I stayed in dying cramps with heat all through my body. I couldn't go to the doctor's appointment because they had me just that bounded. Every time I try to go somewhere. I would have to carry a cup because I was always throwing up. When I did go see the doctor. He immediately had me hospitalized because of the pregnancy. When I was there.

I heard crackling sounds as I was looking at the moon, and then my eyes started to become glossy with water in them. My body started feeling like something was coming over me, and started with a warm aura all around my body. Then I would start throwing up again. This was a horrible first-time pregnancy. Nothing about it was normal.

It went beyond what we call morning sickness. Since Mrs. Acosta couldn't do anything to get it off. We finally parted ways. My mom got in contact with someone in New York. She wanted to see if they could help, and they suggested she bring me there. We had to get money up. So that we would be able to take a plane there. It was just me, and mom. When we arrived.

We met up with my uncle. When he noticed me. His jaw dropped because he couldn't believe his eyes. The condition I was in. I went back to a skeletal frame again while carrying the baby. My baby belly had disappeared. I had lost too much weight to be true. The baby was still alive though just holding on for dear life, but wasn't receiving any nutrition. I wasn't either. That night we stayed at a friend's house close to my uncle.

The middle of the night I woke up hollering. My mom woke up, and called the ambulance. I was taken to the hospital. They wanted to keep me, but I refused. The next day we went to stay down the street from my uncle. I was still feeling lots of burning in my legs, and my organs being pressed down on. No, it wasn't the baby, but the demons that had taken over. The day after I went to see another lady. This lady was strong in witchcraft also.

She saw my condition, and said that the other lady tried to kill me. If I had of listened to her instructions then I wouldn't be here to tell it. This lady was smoking a cigar, and she was blowing smoke right in my face. This lady was very dark skinned, and a thick Haitian accent. She said. I have to get a pigeon and cook it alive. She instructed me to drink it as a remedy. She went on to ask me where was this certain person.

I told her back at home. She then called him a foreign creep. Then went on to say she has something that will get them if I wanted them. I told her. No! I don't want anything done to get him. My thoughts were you talking to me about getting someone, and I'm trying to get me and my baby's life saved. I'm not thinking about anyone right now.

I was done with witchcraft, and witchcraft believers. I didn't want anything to do with that stuff anymore! The following day I was taken to the hospital. I was hospitalized this time, and transferred to another hospital. They took an ultrasound of the baby. I was six months pregnant by this time, and this was the month of June.

I was told the sex of the child was a male. I felt so let down because I was expecting a girl. I didn't want the baby. Then I told my mom she can have him, and take care of him. He would be hers. She could also name him. After the search for help in these different areas. We weren't successful. We were ready to go back home, and we took a bus back instead.

While we took the long route back. I had no symptoms. We made it back safely. I stayed at home at this point, and it seemed as if I just gave up. I didn't know what else to do. I had an exorcism performed by a pastor. A witch doctor practice didn't work. Doctors didn't help. What's left to try? I still couldn't keep much down, and I had done lost a total forty pounds during my pregnancy. I didn't want to try anything like meds or therapy. A week after we came back.

A healthy start nurse came by our house to check on things. She was terribly compassionate at the condition she saw me in. She never saw anyone look like that in all her days with a pregnancy, and she felt pity. She said, "I had stepped into a danger zone, and I needed to be in a hospital." I told her. I didn't want to go because no one could help me. She said. "Something has to be done about this." She said. "You have to go." "I don't know about the baby surviving at this point, but we have to try to save you." I agreed to go to the hospital.

I was admitted when I got there. They put me on a big dose of zofran through the IV. I was in there for three weeks. They were trying to feed me. I still wasn't gaining any weight. The baby wasn't doing any better either. The high-risk doctor came in one morning for me take some meds, but I refused everything they tried to do. He decided. They were going to perform an emergency C-section. Since I wouldn't take anything they offered. They performed the operation, and my baby weighed one pound fifteen ounces and thirteen inches long.

Not to mention two months early. He just became twenty-nine weeks. During the operation I felt everything! I felt them cutting, pulling, and tugging on me. Like they were going to push me off the table. I was in so much pain. I just had tears running out my eyes. I couldn't move, and I couldn't feel my body. As the baby was being removed from my body. I felt a strong force of heat release from my body, and soon after I fell asleep.

I was wheeled to my recovery room. Where I was doing ok for the most part. The baby was out, and I couldn't feel my bottom lower half. My pain was subdued for the time. When I regained my strength, and feeling back I started getting strong cramps in my lower half. It was making me feel so sick. I found out that I hadn't had a bowel movement the whole time I was in the hospital, and they had me on bed rest. The whole three weeks I was on Zofran it was backing my bowels up.

Therefore, I was put at risk for becoming severely constipated to calm my nausea down. I did pass them over the next couple of days all because of God's Grace. My baby was doing way better out than in. He was hanging on strong, and he was even breathing on his own. He was turning his head, and tolerating his nutrition. I also started healing.

I had gain five pounds back in the second week of leaving the hospital. I was eating and thriving again. My little fighter was thriving and growing too. We both was on our way! Thank you, God!! I didn't know how I was surviving all of these encounters, but I was! My baby was in the NICU. He was doing great. I was going to check on him, and sit with him daily. He was in there for six weeks, and thereafter released to go home. I had moved out from my mom, and back in my own place. Me and my sister moved in together. It was supposed to be a fresh start.

I started back communicating with Barracuda. It took an unexpected turn here. I only wanted him to be there for our child not myself. However, my mind was going backwards instead of forward. I begin having feelings for him again. Everything was somewhat going well for me and my little baby. I felt myself becoming very depressed over my life. I actually couldn't see the light in this setting.

However, six months into our new life. I began feeling strange all over again. I didn't know what was going on. Someone suggest I was pregnant again! I didn't know what to think. I was traumatized by my last pregnancy. I said, "I don't want to endure that same experience all over again." I was crying. They told me it may not be the same experience. I did take another test to confirm it. By this time, I believed I was just cursed altogether.

Ch. 5

Consumed by Demons with A 2nd Pregnancy

—— ✝ ——

It was March of 2012. I was very depressed and always crying. I didn't know why. My sister and I went to the store. We went to get slushies for everyone. My sister went to get the drinks, but left me to carry them. I started boohoo crying. I felt so used, and manipulated. She looked at me, and said what's wrong" I said, "You made me carry all those drinks by myself!!" She looked at me very confused. And said, "Huh?" "Really." I said, "Yes!"

She was confused. She said, "Ok." I knew I was terribly sad. I took a test to see if I had conceived a second time. The test results were positive. I was thinking not again! Why me? Why me? Why me? I didn't want anyone to know I was expecting again. I believed they would criticize me. Especially, since it was soon after I had been through torment with the first one. I tried to make this time a positive outlook. I was looking at it from a different view.

I told Barracuda I was going to keep it. He asked me was I sure. My first baby really needed his mother, and they were afraid of this episode claiming my life. It was one night. I had made some roast, and potatoes not even ten minutes after eating. My stomach started clamoring, and hurting. I was screaming, and then began sweating profusely. I sent a text to Barracuda. I ask him to please stop by.

I wasn't feeling well. He came by. I was lying on the sofa. He came over to me. He said, "you are burning up!" I said, "I just ate some roast, potatoes, and my stomach began broiling with heat. He said, "You have it hot in here!" I was sobbing. I said, "I don't feel well." He said, "You going to go to the hospital?" I said, "no!" I told him. "Please! don't leave me alone!" "I feel horrible!"

He laid down on the sofa. I laid next to him with my stomach pressed very securely. It was awkward, but it was comforting to me. I was able to rest as long as I was next to someone. The minute the person would move me. The demons would start torturing me again. For some strange reason the demons were calm when I had a second heartbeat next to me.

Therefore, I got use to lying next to people in this second pregnancy. However, he woke up. He said. He was going to leave, but if it started again, or got worse contact him. I pleaded with him not to leave, but he insisted. That night I was restless, and whining all night long. I called Barracuda maybe twenty-seven times that night. He didn't respond. I didn't know what to do. I was going through it again! I was calling on God because no one else was there. I felt horrible inside and out.

I left that evening, and went to the hospital. I must've sat and waited from 5 pm until 4 am. That was the ER all over again. After leaving. I went to my mom's house. I said, "Here we go again!" This pregnancy went downhill at three months also. All before then everything seemed like it was going to be fine. Was this a coincidence that demons roused up in the second pregnancy as they did the first? Was it just the fact that I just have pregnancies where I'm just meant to be sick?

This was no coincidence, and I'm not prone to being sick with pregnancies. This was demonic possession because of disobedience and sin. I was so sick this time it wasn't a natural morning sickness, and doctors didn't understand it. They just kept calling it extreme nausea. It was many times I plan to go somewhere or do something. I wasn't able to go when time permitted because these forces would attack, and just consume me the whole day from morning to night. The symptoms consist of nausea, strong stomach pains, irritability, shoulder aches, weakness, fatigue, and not able to keep anything in.

I would be able to eat whatever I want for two days straight after that. They would attack from morning to evening for three days straight. I decided I didn't want to go through this any longer. I said, "I'll abort the baby to stop it"! I never been one to believe in this method, but the pain was overbearing. It was five days before my first trimester ended. I went to the hospital because of dehydration, and chronic nausea. They hospitalized me, check the baby's heartbeat, and took an ultrasound.

I informed them I wasn't keeping it. I was going to end it. They said, "Ok, but whatever you decide to do." You don't have long to get it done". They explained the procedure to me. Two days later a doctor came in the room, and said, "Well I heard about your plans so, I don't think you want this. I'm going to leave this right here." He put the ultrasound picture on the table face down, and exited the room.

I just laid there in the bed, and went asleep. I woke up, and somcthing told mc to look at the ultrasound. I picked it up, and glanced at it. I saw my baby with legs, and arms up. I reconsidered because an angel spoke to me, and showed me my first child in my second child. I said, "I can't do it!" There is no way. I told God. "I'm not doing it!" "I'll just fight this me and the baby." "I'll just endure what I have to." "We can make it over this!"

I declared this before I knew it, I decreed and declared this with a warrior spirit that came over me. I called my mom right after, and explained to her that I wasn't going to do it. I'm just going to endure to make it through this. She agreed. She said, "I'm with you." I explained to her why I decided to go this route. After that,

I prepared to leave the hospital to go home. The doctor assigned me to outpatient treatment for IV fluids.

Every Saturday I had to receive infusions to keep my levels up. I went to stay with my mom. Therefore, I wouldn't be alone when they start to attack. They were attacking more at night than day. The attacks at night. I would wake my mom up to lay on her for comfort. It was habitual. The demons had me like a baby. Although, I was carrying a baby. They also were soothed when I would suck a baby's bottle. It was a dramatic stage, but it was real.

I was hospitalized several times in my pregnancy from three and a half months until five months. In that time frame doctors wanted to insert another peg tube in me to feed the baby. I refused it the last time I had it. It was a horrible experience. I said never again. Next, they offered a feeding tube that's inserted through the nose. I accepted it, but it felt horribly uncomfortable, and kept coming out!

I then refused it. They kept trying to plant the peg tube on me, and I wouldn't give in. I told myself not in this lifetime. It made me feel limited when I wasn't. They eventually released me. I went back home. One day a woman of God came to check on me. She prayed as I was crying. I asked her. "What's going on with me?" She responded," "God is angry with you?" I said, "I don't understand what did I do?" I then said. "Whatever I did I'm sorry!"

I was speaking in regret. I kept saying. "I'm sorry." "I'm sorry." "I'm so sorry." Just please make them stop please make them stop. She felt sorry, but there wasn't much she could do. I was going to my treatments on Saturday. Immediately during my treatment. I would feel an attack coming on. The nurse saw the state I was in. She said, "Honey if I was going through all that. I wouldn't let a man come anywhere near me with a ten-foot pole!" After the doctors didn't see me getting well.

They went ahead and hospitalized me at six months. This time it was due to some unfamiliar hemorrhaging. It was the same story. I was hospitalized for the last time. The grace of God. I was doing better toward the end of my pregnancy. Although I was still in the hospital. I was only ninety-one pounds when I entered, but God heard my cry, and strengthened me to bring this baby in the world. I was praying to God while I was there, and this warrior spirit continued with me! This baby appetite increased greatly, and I went from not able to eat at all.

I was eating everything at seven months. I would eat the hospital meals and ask people to bring me food. I would also ask the nurses to bring me all the snacks in the kitchen. I was eating like this all day every day except for when I was sleep. The nausea and vomiting stop except when I would eat too much. The doctor came in with her report and said, "Tyniesha," I'm so proud of you!" "You haven't been throwing up lately!" You and the baby are gaining weight!" I got up to one-hundred twelve pounds in one week.

I didn't realize how fast I was gaining it. My routine considered eating and lying in bed all day. When they came in my room they would weigh me. I told them they have to do it again. Something was off. They said. "No, it's right!" "That's how much you weigh now." I was amazed how fast things were changing for me. I asked them every week.

Can they deliver her now? They said, "We want the baby to stay in as long as possible." All was well by now. Baby was thriving and so was I! The high-risk doctor just wanted to keep me in there. He came in, and gave his report. His words were. "I don't know how on earth you and the baby made it, but you guys are tough as nails!" "Congratulations!" He left out the room.

They decided to deliver the baby at thirty-six weeks. I was so happy. I was ready to get my baby out. It was October 2012. My baby was taken out, and I got to hold her. When I looked at her. I was rejoicing. Everything that I had to endure to get her here. It ended up being worth the fight. I immediately fell in love. I told her, "You were worth it!" She was beautiful. and weighed five pounds five ounces eighteen inches long. We were on our way at this point.

I was discharged from the hospital, and went back to my mom's house. My daughter was released a few days later. I now had two babies. We moved into our new residence. It was fine for the first two months. I then started feeling bad again. I thought I had a stomach virus. It started in the morning. I started feeling a strange vibration all around my body. I didn't know how to deal with it.

I felt spirits closing in on me from every side. I felt depression, weakness, fatigue, lonely, hurt, and sick. It was more like the negative spirits that were closing in on me. They were actually consuming me. The atmosphere I was creating wasn't bringing much life to me. I felt like the walls were closing in on me.

I also was feeling like I was being smothered in a black box. I felt darkness all around. These episodes were taunting me regularly. I would cry hysterically. People normally call it baby blues. This was deeper than that. One morning I woke up very sick. I was so nauseated. I wasn't throwing up. I had pain on one side of my temple. I was just lying in bed most of the day. I was feeling dehydrated. I thought if I ate something.

I would feel better, but I was getting worse. I ate some shrimp earlier that day and that night I felt so bad. I drank a sports drink and threw it up all night long! I was on one sofa, and my friend was there also. He was on the other sofa. We both were sick but two different sickness. I got up at dawn, and rushed to the bathroom.

I had got so dehydrated over-night. I went in the bathroom, and threw up again. Then I fell to the floor, and start screaming. He woke up, and showed concern. He came into the hallway from the bathroom. He said, "what's wrong?" I couldn't talk at this point. He said, "I'm calling the ambulance and you are going to the hospital!"

I was sent to the hospital. Once, again I was given calcium, and potassium. They were severely low. I was there all day until night. I was finally released to go back home. I was fine for a while as for about a month, and then it began to bothering me again. I was at my mom's house, and it start in my stomach.

I thought I had to have a bowel movement. There was nothing moving. My stomach was boiling, and burning in knots. I couldn't get any relief, and the vomiting start all over again. This episode was for a week straight. I didn't go to the hospital this time I stuck it out at home. It did stop eventually.

It was the year of 2013. I was ready to move again. Around late September I moved to my new residence. This was supposed to be a new beginning, and a new location. That was the worse move yet.

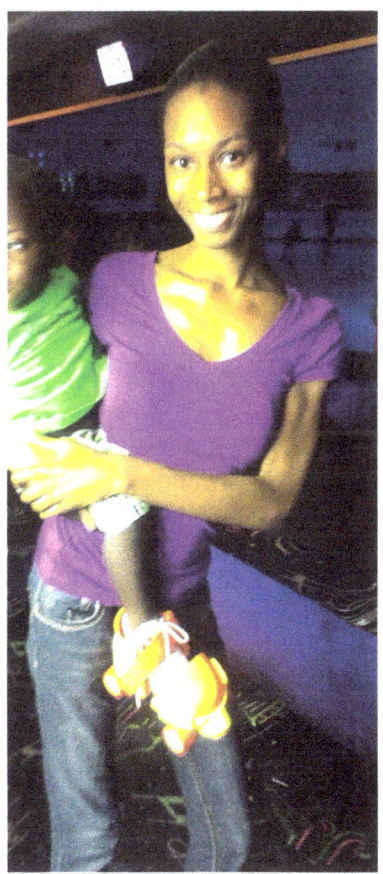

CH.6

The Power of Demonized Territory

I had moved into a new location. I thought things would get better, and stay better. I started going to school again. I thought a new beginning. A new career change or at least picking up where I left off. All was well for a while or was it? The place I chose to live in was a wrong move. It was a friend to the family who was in charge of the house. The thing to that is Mrs. Acosta had been here a couple of times, but I didn't know it was to that extent. I made sure I was avoiding the room she was in. I thought to choose the room opposite from her.

    I should have known, but I didn't. I had a roommate to move into the other room, and she was concerned about a strange circle that appeared on the floor next to the door. It was a perfect circle. It would come and go. For a moment I thought my eyes were playing tricks on me. One night me and my roommate came home from school, and she noticed a big anointed cross on every door as if it were just applied. We didn't understand what we were seeing, or what caused it.

    One day I woke up with pressure on the left side of my temple. It was excruciating, and I didn't understand it. I felt so strange, and a warm tingly sensation was all around me. My roommate came in my room, and asked was I ok. I told her. I think I need to drink something. She said all she had was mountain dew. She gave me that, and I start throwing up. I was crying, and then I start screaming. I was just bearing it. I felt really horrible. It's like someone was just twisting up my intestines. I felt really awful. My roommate became frightened by what she saw, and then she called the ambulance. Once, again I was on my way to the hospital!

The diagnoses returned as constipation, and dehydration. I was very known for this occurrence at the hospital. I had also been told I had acute pancreatitis. I was hospitalized for three days during this episode. The following month or so was fine. I was on my way to school one evening. I felt really bad, but I couldn't cancel out. I had missed the max amount of days. I was in the classroom. My head felt as If someone was just pointing a knife toward my temple. It was always the left side. I held my head down, and tried to rest. My teacher saw my behavior. He asked. "What was wrong?" I told him my head hurts. He suggest. I take something for the pain.

He looked at me with concern in his eyes. It was time for us to go get our client. As I was working on my client. I felt like something was coming over me once again. I continued working. Once I was done. I ran out the room sobbing uncontrollably. I start crying even harder. Next, I began screaming from my soul! It was many people in the school, and I scared every one of them. They excused me for the rest of the night. They had a local student to take me to my mom's house. I remained there for the rest of the night. The same time some work was done at our residence.

The landlord was working on the backyard. He replaced a new pipe under the ground. He been working on it for some time. He left the hole that he dug up open for weeks. Me and my toddlers were going in the backyard. My baby girl found a skull head. She brought it to me. When I realized what she had I made her throw it down. I knew what this meant, but I was hoping it wouldn't get to my child. I went on to behave like it didn't happen, but I felt something was about to be awakened. It taunted me for weeks. I couldn't get away from it. I didn't tell anyone because I knew that the spirits would hear me. I wanted all this demonic work to just go away. It got quiet for a while, and life was moving forward. My first roommate moved out.

I got another roommate and we were good friends. All was fine in the beginning. It was the summer of 2014. Two months after this new roommate moved in. I got extremely sick one morning. I didn't know what was going on. I felt like my organs were on fire. My mom came over that evening to visit. She saw the agony I was in.

She thought some prune juice would make it better. I drank some. I thought the same thing. I waited for about three hours hoping to get my stomach relieved. I decided to go to the bathroom. It felt like someone was pulling on my intestines and tying them up. I was crying at this point. There was no relief from this. I was crying out for help and mercy, but there wasn't any. I was in the bathroom for hours. There was nothing.

It was knots and pulling in my stomach lining. I couldn't sleep. I was being tortured all night long from this pain. The next morning at dawn I started hollering from the bottom of my soul. My roommate came running around asking what's wrong? I told him. "I'm in so much pain!" help me! help me! Please!" He started panicking he didn't know what to do.

He got down at the bottom of my bed because I was curled up sideways, and started pushing on my stomach. It wasn't helping. It was hurting eighty times worse. He called the ambulance, and I was sent to the hospital again. The diagnoses returned as constipation, and nothing more. I was in there for two days, and then released.

I went to my mom's house for the remainder of the week. I returned back home. It was November of 2015. I start working again. I was on my own. I was happy again, and at peace. Me and my children were enjoying life again. Nothing bad was going on. I completed the courses. At work I made a few friends. We would go out to eat.

Hang out afterwards at the mall, and so on. No other episodes occurred for the rest of this time. One day in the Spring of 2016. I went to the beach with my friends. I notice I was losing weight again, and my appetite decreased. This was the last day I was in a happy spirit. It was May of 2016. One day I woke up feeling sick. I was coming down with something.

I wasn't feeling well. I felt a little bloated. I had a weak appetite. That same evening around 6 pm. I start throwing up, and crying. Around 11 pm. at night I start shaking and having cold sweats throughout my body. I began screaming to the top of my lungs. My mom woke up and walked out to the hallway in a frantic and hysterical panic.

She looked quickly down at the floor, and saw me lying in the fetal position. I start crying and holding my midsection. She asked me did I want to go to the hospital. I responded, "No!" then she told me to go get on the sofa. I got up and went in the living room. I got on the sofa, laid down, and fell fast asleep. The next day I woke up. My mom wanted to talk with me. She informed me. She began to think that my past had come back on me. I blurted out in anger. "You really think this is always about that!" "Why would you think that?" I said, "Please don't bring that up again." She quickly stated her claim.

She said, "Well you only seem to behave like that when those demons come upon you!" I thought for a split second. I went on to think otherwise. This couldn't be a haunting from the past or could it! I needed a minute to recollect my thoughts. In the midst of all my past experiences and what they could contain. This would be a bite on the blessed parts of me.

I was starting to go down mentally again. One Sunday morning I went into work early that day. I had a migraine pain on the left side that was pulsating while I was on the phone. It was getting too intense to bear. I had to take a moment out and get a bathroom break to collect myself. It was awful. It wasn't letting up, but only getting worse.

I returned to my seat from my break. My friends were looking from nearby and notice I wasn't feeling well. I looked away to avoid making eye contact with them. They grew concerned as they watched in horror. They discontinued what they were doing and went to consult a supervisor. The supervisor came over. She told me I could leave for today, and I did. I went home and got in the bed. I awoke a few hours later with some relief.

Then I went to my mom's house for the rest of that day. The following week I had an episode of attacks. One evening I had a strong excruciating pain that went throughout my body. I didn't know where it came from, but my whole body was locking up. I couldn't control it, but only scream in horror. My mom said she was calling. The ambulance, and I went to the hospital. They took me into the ER room somewhere. I dreaded going because of my past.

They didn't keep me long. They found me to have negative test results, and exited me out the door. Two days later I had another attack. This time I tried another hospital to see if anything could be determined. Since it was coming from a deeper place than just my mind. I was hospitalized for hours and the doctor seemed perplex to have a diagnosis. She said. She found it to be pneumonia of the lungs. I was relieved that something was found.

That meant there was healing on the way or was it? I left the doctor with many prescriptions. I never had pneumonia before so I just followed through as directed. The pain stopped and I thought everything was all well or so it seemed. A week or so went by and my health started taking a plunge and my appetite had plummeted. I actually found myself becoming uneasy in my skin, and depression was slipping in faster than a stomach virus that has run its course.

My attitude started increasing. One day at work I felt a river like wave plunge through my intestine. My first thought was I had to use the bathroom. When time came to go. I had a pain that was just sitting in my intestines, and felt as if they were on fire, but the pain wasn't subsiding. It literally felt like someone was squeezing my esophagus, and spitting fire on it. I didn't know what in the world to do. I was in the bathroom for hours, and I was sweating fiercely.

The pain still wasn't subsiding. I was crying because I didn't know why I was in so much pain. I finally gave up on trying to pass a bowel movement. I left out the bathroom. I laid down in bed, and fell asleep until the next day. The next day my mind was puzzled as to what was coming upon me. I stopped going to work, and started staying at my mom's house. Things had taken a turn for the worse. I was now under the care of my mom once again. My life had flipped on me, and it wasn't a part of my plans, but it happened. I couldn't fathom what I had done for this to come upon me. I was out of work. This sickness wasn't letting up at all. Day turned into night.

Night turned into day. Time went on and on. Everyone was living their life. I wasn't. I had two children, and couldn't tend to them. What was my life becoming? If this was what my life consisted of. I didn't want to live anymore. It wasn't worth it. I'm a young lady. I'm not fulfilling my life, or my dreams. My life isn't allowing me to get a breather, or an understanding of what hell has awakened in my life again. By this time, everything was a regret. No light was at the end of my tunnel or was it?

CH.7

Redemption by a miracle

✢

It had been months by now. I had been accustomed to my mom's sofa. My day consisted of laying on her sofa and throwing up. People would be in and out the door. I would just lay there with my head turned the opposite direction. It was the most uncomfortable situation I had been presented with. When people would come in the door. I could feel the negative forces coming in with them and it was affecting me greatly.

I felt negative energy all around me. It's like I would feel an attack from an unseen force. No one understood what I was experiencing. There was an unwanted presence that surrounded me. I would try to sleep in the day and I felt bonded with chains. At night I would just be awake at 12 am-6 am. That's when the sun comes up. I couldn't go to sleep if I wanted to. I would just sit up like a dog waiting for something to happen. I couldn't eat or drink.

My mom got tired, and said let's go to the hospital because now you're just wasting away. She said, "You can't continue going on like this!" I responded, "Ok." The next day we went to the hospital and the report returned the same! While at the hospital they decided to setup an appointment with the G.I. doctor. I remained at my mom's house continuing in the same madness until the date. The date came, and I was unable to walk while my mom wheeled me in.

Several Encounters of the Supernatural

They asked a couple of questions, and I pleaded my cause with them. The doctor came in, and told me I can keep something down. Some soups or something lite will stay down. His instructions were to go home, eat some light soup, sit up for two hours, and watch it stay down. The doctor left me feeling worse than ever. I left feeling hopeless and upset. He didn't believe my story! No one did! What was the sense of caring anymore!

I wanted to just go home, and give up! I got home, and I questioned my belief in myself. I started to think that I wasn't sick and that I had done lost my mind. Then a small voice whispered, "Ask about the pastor." I asked my mom since the doctor couldn't find anything. Do she think her pastor could come over to see if he saw anything! She agreed, and attempted to reach out to him. She was able to contact him. He was on his family vacation at the time he was contacted.

He agreed to come over. It was about 10:30 pm that same night when he arrived. He arrived with three others who he called a part of his entourage. They came in first and made cordial conversation with my mom. I was laying on the sofa sideways facing the entrance door. They were just looking at me, but talking to my mom. Then the pastor came into the door. He walked over and sat on the sofa. He was speaking and observing at the same time. He was very spiritual and could see into the spirit. He preceded to talk directly to me.

Tears started strolling down my face. I became so emotional in his presence. He stood up, and came near me like he was going to lay hands on me. I immediately started squirming backwards, and hit the floor! I was moving like a serpent literally! They caught me, and held me down. I was howling like a demon. His entourage eyes grew big in horror. They couldn't believe what they were up against. They first thought they was coming to pray for a sick individual.

Redemption By A Miracle

They had no idea their fight was going to be with actual full-grown live demons. They were praying, and calling them out. It ended up being a night wrestling with the enemy. I couldn't believe myself what was revealed in me. They were not successful with casting them down on the first night. They were fighting for me. I was completely exhausted. There was no fight in me. They had taken complete control over me.

The pastor was a true man of God. He was one after God's own heart. I never knew of this around this time in my life. These people didn't give up on me! Regardless of what it looked like. They stayed right by my side. I didn't have much understanding. The pastor determined that these demons were too strong for him alone. He knew that strength came in numbers, and he reached out to other pastors for help.

No one wanted to take on the responsibility of helping with deliverance. They all feared of them being consumed by the demons. I also had no love at this time, and it was very dark in my life. They were telling me the reason for this happening was because I had no word in me. I was very confused as to what that had to do with anything.

They also told me to confess by my mouth that Jesus Christ is Lord, and I believe he was sent for my sins. I repeated what they said, but I didn't believe it. I wanted them to leave me alone. I didn't understand the method to what they were doing. I was sorrowful, and hopeless. I just wanted relief in whatever way possible.

However, these people would come get me on my worst days, and take me to church! I would be throwing up with stomach pains! It was harsh at church the demons would show up more than ever and I would be in the fetal position most of the time. I had a baby bottle that I kept close to me. I would be in church going into convulsions, screaming, shaking, foaming from the mouth, and the works. The pastor would tell me what to say to the Lord at the altar.

I would do it, and just be crying hysterically. I felt so helpless! The pastor wanted to see the process sped up for deliverance. He decided to try help in another area. The catholic church, since he had heard of them specializing in exorcism. This definitely was a special rare case for it. He looked into Catholic priest, and came across one online.

My mom called and set up the appointment. I got to go visit, and see what could be done. They had a date setup. The day arrived when they went to the church to setup a home visit. They set the date for a visit on Friday. Everyone made proper arrangements to be present. My mom, sister, pastor's entourage, and pastor.

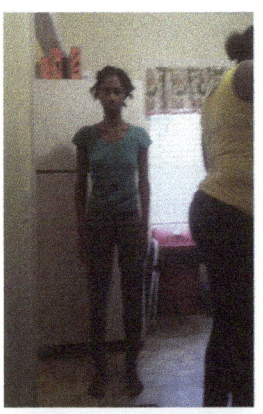

The two Catholic priests also were on hand. I was laying on my stomach on the sofa. I was bounded so I couldn't respond, but I could hear everything! The demons had me where I couldn't speak or move. My head was always turned away from people. They had sheets of paper they handed out for everyone present to recite. They had a bottle of holy water. They had an item in hand.

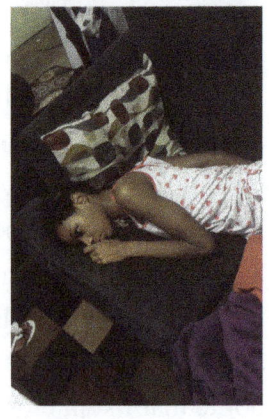

They were reciting the words very softly from the paper, and dabbing the item. This was done with little to no authority! Everyone just sat around waiting to see something happen, but nothing happened. My sister had compassion for me. She started to speak out of order with authority! She wanted her sister free from the torment. Everyone had to calm her down. She was hitting me in the face. She wanted them to release me. They finally stopped the exorcism. They said, "We would have to return for another session." They knew once they were gone.

They wouldn't be back! They didn't know what they were doing, or what they were up against! The pastor ruled that out no. He still was on the look for a breakthrough. He also told me that God was going to deliver me, but he wanted Glory himself.

I only understood part of this prophecy. God was going to deliver me. Time went on, and this gruesome sickness consumed my day, my night, and my life. Nothing had changed until one night. God started speaking to me. He said, "Tell me what's wrong? and what you want me to do for you?" I found myself talking to the Lord strictly from my heart.

I wasn't holding back anymore! I wasn't in disbelief. I talked to the Lord for many hours that night. I would tell him exactly how I felt, and what I needed done. He was listening. I started to see a change in the nature of my condition. That's when I saw God was real, and had all power to change my situation. I went from symptoms that went on for days, and nights.

Next, I get relief by reading his word, and talking to him. I started to understand what the pastor meant. When he said, "I was defeated because I had no word in me." The more I read the more I gained strength to fight what was fighting me. I came to understanding that Jesus was the way, the truth, and the light. I used the word to speak and use authority toward demonic forces. They didn't have the power they once possessed over me.

I was attending church regularly, fighting for my life, and attending every service that we had. They were still present, but losing strength. The Pastor went through another contact to fight these demonic vulgar forces. This was a woman of God and she was a woman after God's own heart. She agreed to help fight these forces. She spent time before God seeking him. She was preparing herself for battle. She invited us to her church.

She had it set up for deliverance. She had a congregation that was praying in tongues, and she had me to speak by mouth. Every demon she saw present and renounce them. She then anointed me with oil, and spoke against what we were up against. I felt so exhausted after the exorcism experiences. I wanted to just go to bed.

I never knew what it was like to have to fight such strong forces. It was no joke, and definitely out of our control. God had this battle with him, so he was the only one who could save me, or get me free. My constant time at church, and in God's word start to have a dramatic impact on my life as a whole. My mind started changing on how I viewed things.

My heart even changed, and I decided to give my life to God. He performed the miracle that no one could. My miracle happened in November of 2016. I decided to join the church, and speak about what God had done for me. The pastor, and his entourage showed me love like I never known anyone to ever have. They barely knew me, yet they stuck by me through my worsts time. Treat me as one of their own children. Their level of compassion spoke volumes to me.

They never gave up on me. Regardless of how it appears. At the time that the pastor, and his entourage came to me. I looked like a gaunt dog. It was death itself, and everyone else was scared to fight. I just didn't know what in the world to do. I grew to know God for what he had done. I was happy that my breakthrough came. I still felt a void like something was wrong. I was unhappy in a different way. I didn't understand why I felt so lonely, and empty. I had my new found love for Christ spiritually, but naturally I felt different.

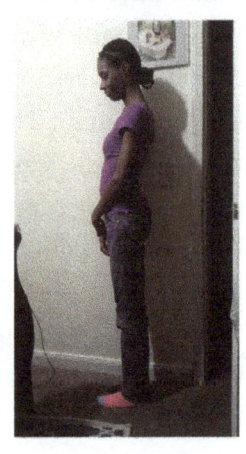

I was around my sister and her mate at the time. I felt maybe I hadn't had a friend or companion in a year. I watch them have fun, and play together. I felt this is what I was missing. I did become friends with someone. I just didn't want to be alone. I start hanging with this person. I was happy with this person for a moment. It was like a slip away from reality. I would talk to this person, and trust them to talk back.

This person talked about Jesus and God. I thought if he loved God then he understood me. I couldn't be anymore wrong. It wasn't going where I thought it was. I found myself slipping away from God, and going back to my old ways. This was a wrong turn! I hung with this person. I started to do things I normally don't do and I wasn't happy with this. This was the worst dead end I ever put myself in. All this person talked about was fornication.

I learned that wasn't where my heart was. I noticed my aura changed, and now I had lusting spirits on me. They were crowding my space. They were making me feel hot all over, and they were back again! I didn't know what hit me. I went downhill again! The next day which was in the month of April 2017. I got into a car accident where I was the driver, and was T-boned.

My kids were in the car with me. I was so shaken up, and my wrist was on fire at least it felt like it. I went to the hospital. They took x-rays of my hand and back. I was released a few hours later. I went to my sister's house where my mom was. She was in the living room and I was sick again. I didn't understand what caused this to return

. I went back to the pastor. I asked him what is going on with me. He stated. I went left again somewhere down the line! I didn't understand what that meant. He also said, "Just because you fight the devil off doesn't mean he wouldn't come back!" He still showed a heart of compassion and tried to help me again. He had me to come to the church, and anointed me. He prayed over me. He said I had one foot on the earth, and one foot in the grave.

I was regretful of what had this to return. I was back in the fetal position. I was back at my mom's house, and I was going through it all over again. I was just enduring this pain all over again. It was with me night and day. This time though I was done for real. I had changed my life again. I was seeking God for myself. I was taking the route talking to God.

Praying for myself, reading his word, and participating in services. I used everything I learned the first time to fight this time. Pastor even made a few appearances in this season when I was sick again. This time the Lord wanted me to prove it to him that I wanted to be free from demons. This episode lasted for about three months straight.

One morning I awoke in tears and it was the month of July 2017. I was talking to God. He reminded me of every time. He delivered me from something abnormal. I didn't realize. It was him. The whole time! I immediately started crying for his mercy, and grace. He had placed over me. I also had a desire in my heart to touch his feet. I read the new testament I became intimate with the stories where others were right there with Jesus.

They touched him, and were healed from demonic experiences. I wanted an encounter like that one because I believed I could get healed with one touch of him. The story with the woman with the issue of blood I became fond of. She had been sick for twelve years. She had been to every doctor and nothing healed her.

She was in a crowd of people that was in line to be touched by Jesus. She thought, "if I could just touch the hem of his garment I would be healed!" She did touch him, and he felt his power go from him. He looked and said, "Who touched me?" The woman came forward, and told him it was her. She told him why she did it. He told her to go in peace her faith has made her whole (Mark5:25) I begin to have faith in the same manner, and I actually say the reason for my healing was in a similar manner.

Redemption By A Miracle

I was speaking to God in a universal language one morning, and I continue to listen to a song called before the throne. The song mentioned kneeling before the feet of the King in his presence. I continue to sing this song, while wide awake walking around. I then saw the appearance of an angel in a cloud. He was dressed like he was ready for battle.

He had an armor for clothes on, and a pair of long white wings. Then I saw a pair of gates like the pearly gates, and these were in the clouds. Then the gates opened from the inside. I then saw a pair of feet. They were huge, and I was kneeling down before them. I was like the size of an ant compared to these feet. I saw two legs that were in the position when someone is sitting down in a chair, and I could see their attire from the legs down it was a white robe.

It had the bottom legs and feet revealed, but nothing else. I spoke. "If only I could touch your feet." and he allowed me to touch his feet! I realized this was the feet of God when I touched them! Then I saw the throne in full view! His glory which was the brightest white light or glow I ever seen. It had come off the side of his throne, and shone directly on me.

I realized I reached heaven and had my first physical encounter with Jesus. I was over joyed. I was overwhelmed, and I felt his true love. I had never felt anything like this in my entire life! I had never imagined anything like this would happen to me! When I came to. I wanted to tell everyone what had just happened. I start by telling my mom.

She said, "Oh wow really that's interesting!" Then I told my sister. She said. "If that's true then you shouldn't be sick anymore!" I responded. I don't know! I did learn that this sickness was over from that encounter. I was able to eat again, sleep again, and live again. The demonic sickness had come to an end and I didn't feel that empty and loneliness anymore! It was all over and I felt redeemed and in love with my new found love.

I wasn't seeking for people anymore. I was seeking God and God alone. He was my new true love. That point on my life was never the same again. I had given up the things I use to do completely. I surrendered my life to Jesus Christ wholeheartedly and live for him. He had done the unbelievable, unthinkable, and impossible! I owe him everything for watching over me, protecting me, and keeping me through the many times I put myself in death's shadow.

Ch. 8

Roots from the beginning: A Shocking Revelation sent from heaven

---

All was well at this time in my life. It was quiet and my season of worshipping God was in full bloom. I found myself alone a lot, but I wasn't complaining. This is what God was doing for me. I started understand prophecy more, and the language of God. It was totally different from the views of the World. I became more compassionate toward people.

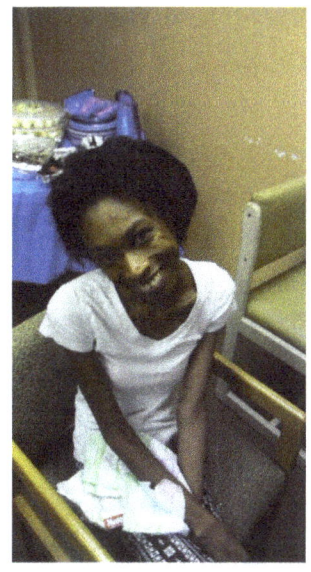

I became more forgiving at heart. My focus was completely on the things of God. God had done changed me from inside out. My appearance changed and God showed me he was pleased with me. I received my health and strength back. I was witnessing about Christ and giving my testimony so others could understand why we serve God alone.

My love was restored. I had strength I never possessed before. Although the enemy would try to upset me. I would keep standing on the word of God. I stopped listening to worldly music. I started listening to music that only promoted the word of God.

It was a sacrifice but every time I was obedient God rewarded me. It was well worth it. My mom moved from the place where she was staying when all the demon sickness was present. Everything felt so beautifully new. I had joy that I couldn't explain. I loved the change that came upon me and my family. I never had my dad around and it always had a huge effect on me.

I always desired to see my dad. I wanted to have him with me. Sometime before I came to know God. I wanted to contact my dad and show him things. I even attempted several times to find him. I had no luck. I even received news that he died. It really ate at me because I never got that chance I desired. I told my children I wouldn't keep their dad from them.

I don't want them to feel what I felt! There were even times when I contemplated suicide because I felt my life would be different with my dad. It's something I never understood. The date was December 25, 2017. My uncle from upstate contacted my mom. He was speaking with her and decided to tell her something. He was very familiar with my dad.

He told my mom that my dad had a bad reputation. He was a mean and hateful man. He even ran a brothel back in his time. His wife at the time was a Madam over the brothel. My dad believed in witchcraft and even put his hands in it. My dad also had blood on his hands because he had murdered someone before.

This was revealed to me and I was so overjoyed not because of the hateful lifestyle he lived but because all my questions that I held inside and never had an answer for how now become a closed case for me. God gave my heart, my mind, and spirit peace from all of this. I learned God wasn't being mean to not let me have my dad. He was protecting me all this time from my dad. In his perfect timing he revealed it. This could have been revealed before, but God saved it for when he knew I could handle it.

It closed many portals to demonic entities having access to me. Generational curses plague our bloodline. We don't have to be sex addicts, drug heads, alcoholics, or witchcraft workers. It doesn't matter what curse threatened your family. Even if it comes it doesn't have to consume us like it did them. This was so clear to me and couldn't be any clearer.

God also showed me that the reason all of this happened was because of my own unclean hands. I was God's anointed vessel, but I was very disobedient to his will for my life. He kept knocking. I wasn't answering and he was saddened by me avoiding him. He then became angry because I wasn't hearing him or seeking him.

I chose a bad path for myself and it caused everything to go against me because I ran from God. I also worshipped other gods, put others before him, and that caused his wrath to come upon me. He allowed me to feel the pain I caused him. He did what he had to do to get my attention. Afterward I learned my lesson and now I fear him.

I learned obedience is better than sacrifice. I was healed and my wounds were now closed. I now saw God as my daddy literally. Everything he gave me access to and performed just for me. He gives me the gift of life. I now understood why people said God was like a mother and father to them. It's when we become intimate and gain personal relationship with him.

He opens our mind to things we didn't know exist. He shows us love like no one can. He transforms our mind from things of the world. He draws us near to him so that we can see what he sees and feel what he feels. People turn to drugs, sex, and alcohol to hide their pain. If we start giving that energy over to God so he can work it out. That's when we can feel his glory and none of the things of the world can take you to that level. It's something you don't want to come down from. I experienced his glory and it changed me completely.

Ch. 9

A 2nd Affliction: A different kind of testimony

Time went on and I continue to walk close to Jesus and be like him. One day around January 2018. I woke up feeling a weird aura around me. I went to the bathroom. I then went to lay down because I wasn't feeling well at all. Affliction hit me so hard. I questioned my situation wondering if I went against God. I needed to know what I did! I thought I was doing everything he wanted me to!

Why did this hit me? The enemy was mad because I no longer served him, but now served God alone. God let me know it wasn't him. This demon was attacking hard. I went to the hospital to see what was wrong. The report came back couldn't find anything. This episode lasted for three months. I was unable to work or get off my sick bed. I lost twenty pounds this time and I became very weak.

While I was enduring this pain. God showed me leaving town without my mom. I had little understanding of what this vision meant. One day at church I went to the altar. I asked God to please don't let me return to the same condition I just came out of. I'll do what you want me to do! I said this sobbing hysterically feeling scared that history was repeating itself.

I never stopped serving God. I would still pray to him and stay before him.I wouldn't allow myself to believe God had brought me this far to leave me. I didn't understand, but I kept telling God I trust him. I learned it wasn't meant to take me out. It was a test of faith. One night while crying out to God. I told him if he had me to go to another state I'll go!

When I prayed the sickness stopped just like that. God had revealed the vision of me being without my mom. He had chosen me to travel from the curse grounds of my home town and go where he was sending me. God told me he would make all things new for me with obedience. He wouldn't allow Satan to ever touch my intestines again.

The sickness wouldn't allow me to eat or drink. I was feeling so miserable. I felt sorry for myself. I felt like I can't enjoy my life. I just wanted to feel God's glory. I knew sickness or depression couldn't go into the presence of God. That's where his glory is. I was constantly throwing up at night and feeling fire like pains in my lower stomach area.

I would wake up around 9 am and by 10 am sickness would start, and a liquid foamy bubbly substance would be running from my mouth. Nothing was easing the pain or stopping it. It would last all night long at times. I would get two complete days of relief and the third day it would start right back around. No one could explain these symptoms or episodes!

I told God I would go because souls had to be saved. I'm just that dedicated to God. God stopped the symptoms and gave me two weeks to prepare for transition. I thought I would have time to get money up and drive my vehicle. I was so wrong! God was really testing me to see how much I trusted him. I was thinking I may lose my one opportunity to get my breakthrough. However, my pastor told me I can still catch the flight out. I quickly said, "I want to go now." I stepped out on faith with little funds and clothes. My kids stayed with my mom because I was going to get established, and send for them later. His word says if you put anything before him.

You're not worthy of him. I put everything aside and left. It was March 2018. I was starting on my journey and God miraculously healed me again! I was in survival mode. I normally eat a certain way but that way wasn't available to me. I had to eat what was available, and it was all microwaveable food. Normally one would say eat healthy to get strength and weight.

I ate microwave foods and I thrived well. I gained weight and my strength wasn't my own, but God's strength that helped. I became strong and healthy. I was the happiest I ever been in my whole life. I was seeking God regularly and it showed. God humbled me in so many ways. I now didn't take anything for granted anymore. God had done broke me down.

He molded me and made me over through these trials I had to face. He taught me that he is my everything. He has power to do everything no matter what people say. Every meal I receive I give him praise. I give him praise even for little things because it lets me know he is thinking about me. I know better than to complain because God gives and God takes away.

God was restoring everything the demons had taken from me. I started back working, living, and enjoying the will of God. Everything was on track and I was happy to meet people and see faces. I love to encourage people. I had a brand-new outlook on life and the creation of God. I'm grateful every day regardless of what situation I'm faced with. I have new found confidence that comes from God. At this time, I was encouraging people and praying for souls.

Several Encounters of the Supernatural

I had been working for a few months now. My job nature changed and I wasn't so zeal about it anymore. I was seeking God about restoring my passion for it, but God just removed me from the job altogether. I wasn't discouraged I was still joyful. I kept my word with God telling him I trust his plan. This date was around October 2018.

I was unemployed around November. 2018. One night I was asleep and I felt a strong heat force hit me in the stomach. It woke me up out of my sleep. I felt it feel strong and a lot of pressure. I began to get a feeling of nausea and sickness. It was December 2018. I also had a strange feeling in my neck. I thought it was a crook from sleeping the wrong way.

It start to hurt whenever people would hug me. It was so much pain I want to cry. I would just brush it off though. One morning I woke up with harsh pains in my stomach. I thought I was coming down with something. I thought it was evil spirits attacking at first. I used the power God gave me to get it off. It went away momentarily. The next morning,

I woke up with the same symptoms. I had a headache, throat pain, stomach pains, and vomiting a slimy liquid substance no food. It was too much and it wasn't letting up. I decided to go to the hospital. I was thinking something would have been found. I arrived at the hospital and they asked me about my history. They ran all kinds of test.

They had me admitted because my main concern was my stomach. I also had lost lots of weight again. This was around a week and a half after symptoms started again. I was too dehydrated because I couldn't get anything in. There was no diarrhea. The stomach pains just wouldn't stop. They released me from the hospital. I returned home with nausea meds. Their ruling was they didn't see anything. My first thought was this couldn't be the attack of evil spirits again. I questioned God and said how am I supposed to get the word out about you if this has returned again.

The symptoms didn't stop at all. They actually got worse. I just laid in bed all day and night. I was just enduring this pain with no mercy. I tried to sleep my life away. I cried, sobbed, and balled up. There were a very few days that I was ok. On those days I would talk to God and worshipped him. I would separate myself from everything and everyone.

I would cry to him a lot because I didn't understand why this came upon me. At first, I thought why would God have me to go through this. Then he spoke and let me knew it wasn't him. I realized that the enemy had access to me. He was doing this and then I saw enough change to make my petition known unto God. It was times I felt like God had left me all alone. Other times I was very emotional. Other times I called on the name of Jesus because I was just enduring all of it. I had no rest and I was throwing up like every 10 minutes.

There were too many restless nights to count. I had pain I didn't know existed. I felt like a knife was stabbing me in my stomach repeatedly. My body was off balance. Nothing was operating as it should. I lost thirty-five pounds in two months. I'm small in stature. I lost all my muscle mass. I was a skeletal frame again. This went on for five months straight. One night I was in mega pain. My neck pain now was constant. My body ached.

I was at my breaking point. I literally cried out to God and said, "I give up!" I can't bare this anymore!" You said, "You would send help!" "Where is my help?" I was up all night long. I was begging for mercy, or just take me. I was ready to die. I thought if this is all my life consisted of and no enjoyment. Please take me. I gave up on doctors because I got tired of hearing, "they can't find anything!" The very next morning around 7 am.

My mom came in the room and said, "You bothered me all night long from your crying and agony." "What's wrong with you?" I explained it to her. She then got a pail and placed it next to me with blankets. She left me alone and the kids went to school.

She returned a few hours later. She came to where I was and said, "Come on, you can't go on like this!" "Do you want to go to the hospital?" I blurted. "No!" I just want to die! She said come on let's go to the hospital.

Pastor is here. I immediately had fear to come over me. I asked her who is that and she said pastor! I knew then God answered my prayer. My pastor was nine-hundred miles away on a business assignment. They popped up on us unaware and unannounced. I knew God had me on his mind. He sent them. My spiritual sister heard what I said. She said, "Oh no ma'am we don't quit!" "You can't fight if you don't have strength."

I didn't even know she was in the room. She used her authority. She said, "Come on let's go to the hospital!" This time was about February 2019. I gave in as she walked me down to the car. I had no mental, physical, or spiritual strength. I barely could stand up straight on my own. I was completely depleted. I went to the hospital once again.

They hospitalized me for loss of excessive weight and stomach problems. They finally managed to get my pain under control with the IV meds. I prayed to God. I asked him to please let them find something. I believed if they had a diagnosis. They could get me the right treatment and cure for me. They repeated the CT scan of the abdomen. They did find missing bone on my hip region. They couldn't find much in the stomach that caused the pain. They did work harder this time than last time. The next day my spiritual family, and my mom came to the hospital. My mom was very concerned. They said they weren't finding much. She asked, them about the hard lump in my breast. They were unaware and ordered a biopsy for tissue samples.

I mentioned my neck because it was in excruciating pain. At first, he said it was because my body nutrition levels were extremely low. He then decided to get an X-ray to buy time. When he did the X-ray. He found a spontaneous fracture. He didn't know the cause of it. He then ordered an MRI of my neck. He found a tumor that caused the fracture. The tumor was a nice size and extended from my c3 to my c6. It was wrapped around my artery.

They then sent the oncologist and I automatically knew that was a cancer doctor. Then I got scared because he said there a huge problem with your neck. Next, the neurologist came in and said, I have to perform surgery on your neck. I was so scared and confused. I know surgery is always a bad thing to me. I went from nothing's wrong to a major surgery has to be performed. After all this scary news was delivered to me. It hit me all at once!

I now needed support and encouragement like never before. This was unexpected and brand new to me. The doctor told me the reason he decided to perform the surgery. He said the bad outweigh the good. If it wasn't done then I would have a stroke or face being paralyzed from the neck down! I immediately called my mom in tears.

I explained the situation to her, and she was compassionate. She then started reaching out to others for prayers to be lifted up. My mom informed my pastor on the update of my status. He was heartfelt and immediately went into prayer. We now had many prayers going up. I was grateful for everyone who took time out to lift my name before the throne of God!

Time was drawing near for my surgery to be done. It was scheduled for the a.m. My pastor reached out to me, and told me to let my petition be known before God. He told me to tell God exactly what I wanted to do for me. I did as he instructed me to do. I actually was talking to God exactly what I wanted him to do for me. I did as he instructed me to do.

I actually was talking to God several times that morning. It was time for my surgery. They rolled me to the back of the OR. They proceeded to dress me for the procedure. The doctor came and talk to me. He told me he was going to place an incision on the front of my neck, completely remove the bone, and replace it with a metal plate and screws.

It will hold my c-spine together. I asked him, "will fixing my neck problem stop my vomiting. "He responded, "No! that is a whole new problem." I looked disturbed. I thought this would fix my most gruesome issue. He also said that if he can't complete it through the front incision. He may have to do a second one through the back of my neck.

The doctor was a little concerned. I looked like any day I could be buried. They took me to the area where the procedure was going to be performed. They put an oxygen mask on my face. The rest was history. I woke up in recovery, and I was so out of it. I didn't know what hit me! The doctor came in with a huge smile on his face. He was pleasantly happy about the outcome. Everything went smoother than he thought. I knew God's angels were in the room with me because I too was very happy.

That's the power of prayers. Prayer changes things! I was in the hospital for two and a half weeks. The first night after my surgery. My throat was very irritated. I didn't get any rest at all! I had a tube connected from the inside of my throat flowing through the outside of my neck. I felt like I couldn't catch my breath at times. Someone was suffocating me!

It was the most uncomfortable experience yet. I was literally calling for meds every few hours. I couldn't get to my meds that I really needed. For medical reasons I was just miserable all the way around. I was so emotional because of the state I was in. It was horrible to me. I was just enduring all of this, and had strength to bear it.

It wasn't my strength, but God who had given me a spirit of confidence through all of this. I knew who was on my side. It was for his glory. I kept lifting my hands, and telling him I trust his plan. Every time I did this. He filled me with reassurance of the original promise. The second night the test results for my breast biopsy came back. It was positive for metastatic breast cancer. It was time to go home. I was waiting on the doctor's assignment.

The radiation doctor came in the room. He explained his plan to start radiation treatments. I asked him. What stage breast cancer did I have?" He responded, "They didn't tell you?" I nervously responded, "No!" his response let me knew it wasn't good. He then said, "They didn't tell you?" again. I responded with the same answer, "no!" He then gave me a surprise smirk on his face. (He said in a brace yourself for this voice) Stage 4(I was like oh wow! that's an advance aggressive stage, and close to the end) those were my thoughts.

He then explained in detail what is expected in this stage, and pretty much tried to influence my thoughts of life expectancy wasn't looking too promising. He actually upset me to even try to put that in my head! My thoughts were your science may say that, but my God is the one who is in control of when the lights get turned out. I was released and went back to my mom's house.

I had a neck brace on. I had to wear it for six weeks straight! The first night at home. I was really sick. There was no ending to throwing up! I was feeling very uncomfortable with the neck brace on. I had to remove it in the middle of the night! I was like my goodness! Will this ever cease?! I literally was in and out the bathroom every three-four minutes.

Every little thing was emptied out of my stomach, and I was still going! I was also in pain. I had to endure these stomach pains I never knew existed! The pain had me balled up crying out in agony! Nothing was stopping it. I cried out Oh my gosh. I didn't know what on earth to do. The pain meds, or nausea meds weren't changing a thing.

I was in this pain the whole time I was at home! My spiritual family stopped by one night to check on things. As they entered the room their hearts fell. They were really moved by the agony they saw me in. They wish they could have a magic touch, and make

Several Encounters of the Supernatural

it all go away! Unfortunately! That wasn't an option! It was all in our master's hands!

Pastor prophesied that this sickness wasn't unto death. He knew it was just the process God was taking me through. I had two stories that was keeping me encouraged. My pastor's daughter who had a similar trial herself, and she made it through the grace of God. The other story is the story of Job in the bible. I was told I had been considered by God. I told God. "Ok Lord, have your way." I began to realize what it took to be a witness of a testimony. I had to go through everything that came along with it. The emotions, the pain, as well as the endurance.

I cried because I felt alone, and no one was going through it, but me! God removed his glory because then I would know what it feels like to not have it! It's horrible not having it. I wanted it back! However, there was nothing fun or happy about the process. It's horrible not having it. I wanted it back! There were times when I couldn't pray. It wasn't there.

I could just call on the name of Jesus, and ask for him to help me get peace, and rest in my body. I then would name each body part, and command it to line up with the word of God. I then find myself drifting off to a peaceful sleep. One day I woke up in dire pain. I was gripping the cover and crying out, "Someone help me, please! please! please!"

The meds I was given wasn't strong enough. My pastor stopped by and asked if I wanted to go to the ER. I went back to the hospital, and they changed my dosage. I was released from the ER a few hours later. I was under the impression of IV meds. The vomiting was under control as long as I was at the hospital. When I got home the throwing up syndrome returned.

I came in the house, and went straight to the bathroom. Afterwards I went upstairs to get in bed. The next two days the nurse from the doctor's office called to check scheduling. She heard my cry in the background. She told my mom she wasn't trying to get in her business, but is that your daughter I hear crying like that?! My mom responded, "Yes! That's her!"

The nurse then said, "Oh my! what is she taking?" My mom said, "Nothing, she saying she wants to be admitted in the hospital." The lady was touched by the sound of my voice. She told my mom, she would reach out to the doctor herself, and see what can be done! She can't be laying there like that in pain, and nothing being done about it.

The nurse called back an hour later. She informed my mom to take me back to the ER, and call the doctor when she arrived. My mom did as she was instructed. I was hospitalized that night for pain, and unable to thrive without nutrition. I had heard of others having cancer, but I didn't see myself as one day having a trial with it! While, I was in the hospital my mom and children were coming to keep me entertained. I started my radiation treatment while in the hospital.

They also started me on TPN since my nutrition levels were extremely low. I still couldn't stop throwing up. The TPN is when they place an extended catheter through the vein in the arm. They do this to feed a malnutrition person who can't take food in the normal way. They also scheduled me for ten days of radiation.

When I was in the hospital the nurse came to take my temperature. It was up to 100.2! This started hitting me at eleven p.m. at night. The nurse came to check on me two hours later, and my temperature climbed up to 102. The nurse then gave me tylenol to break my fever. They knew something was wrong because my temperature kept climbing.

They were very bothered by my temperature rise. They immediately contacted infectious disease doctors. That day I felt horrendous! I had sweats, fever, and chills that just wouldn't quit. My nurse came in the room. She was very sweet and caring. She would alternate every four hours between my meds. They also had me on ten different types of antibiotics. Doctors were coming in throughout the day. They were questioning me about what I was experiencing. I didn't feel like talking to anyone. The symptoms were lasting all day.

My nurse was really patient with me. She noticed my original meds weren't changing the situation. She put in an order to get different meds to work against my symptoms. The symptoms stopped around 12 a.m. that night. I finally start feeling relief. Thank God! I can't do anything without him! I was on antibiotics for a week.

One evening my mom came to the hospital to bring my bible. She knew how much I love my bible. I hold it close to me. I treat it very personal as my very best friend. I don't like to read any other bible. One night while I was alone. I decided to read the story of Job. I thought since everyone says my story reminds them of Job. As I started reading.

I was drawn into Job's world. I saw the revelation and similarities between the thing's Job faced, and the things I was going through. Some of the symptoms were even the same. I felt myself getting strength and things changing. Once I started reading. I couldn't stop! I was reading the story of Job until it was completed. My symptoms started calming down, and weren't as aggressive.

I completed my radiation treatments I was released to go home after two and a half weeks. I decided that I would be obedient if I really wanted to overcome this mountain. It was a sacrifice, but it was well worth it. I said, I'm going to do whatever they tell me to, and take all my meds. I lifted my hands, and told the Lord I trust his plan.

I don't believe he brought me this far to leave me. My faith was in the treatments, meds, and plans that they decided to follow. I was seeking God in prayer, and ask him to lead me, guide me, through this season. After praying I trusted I was in the hands of the Lord. I didn't have access to all the special remedies people have believed to be their cure.

Cannabis oil, change in diet, special plants that people seek to get. I couldn't even get anything in my system. Nothing would stay down! My situation was completely in the hands of God. I had previous experiences where my problem was completely impossible for anyone to change. My worsts demon was the nausea and vomiting.

I would get on the prayer line, and ask everyone to pray for the nausea, vomiting to stop because it was causing me to be miserable. I knew there was strength in numbers. God's word says when two or more are gathered together in his name. God is in the midst. The prayer line is a miracle and breakthrough. It would happen once a week.

People from all over would gather together over the phone. They would give their testimony, story, and praise report of what God had done for them. Its designed to help people who are in need of encouragement and strength, Prayer is then offered up to God about what they need him to do for them. It changed lives and held a lot of power!

There were many times it changed my situation, and therefore I was a firm believer in the prayer service. The date was April 2019. My uncle came into town to spend time with us. I was very thin so I didn't think I would be able to enjoy his visit. He stayed with us for six days. Every day was a new day and full of adventure! I would wake up. Then I would pray and do devotion.

Next, I would eat and take my meds. I would pray

over my meds because I believe they can't do anything without God's grace and healing power! I actually had no symptoms while we were out enjoying life! I thank God that I was able to get out, and eat again! I actually had the most fun while he was around.

I kept thinking about the next week that sickness was going to return, and that I would have to start receiving chemotherapy! I also didn't notice that all my throat pain from the surgery had vanished. My uncle was taking us out to eat every day. I was excited to eat and everything was staying down! It was processing through natural functioning again!

I was actually afraid of my future because that sickness was so horrible once it stopped. I didn't want it to return! The next week came, and I actually didn't receive chemotherapy, or the sickness didn't return either. I started back gaining weight, and didn't notice it. I was going to the doctor and they would weigh me. The number was going up.

I learned God was hearing me and healing me when I least expected it. I didn't realize God was going to answer my prayer while I was thinking otherwise. Another month had gone by and the sickness still didn't return. I was still receiving nutrition from my PICC line as well. It was used only at night, and at morning I would unhook it. It was a very uncomfortable situation.

My faith is in God with every symptom and situation I had to face. Therefore, I replaced complaining and mumbling with praise for God! I had to keep telling God I trust him and his plan as I raised my hand. Now I knew that all treatments and decisions that came about were orchestrated from God. It is the plan of God that is playing out in my life.

I believe with everything that is in me. I knew who was in control of my situation. The sickness was gone. My health and strength were returning. I'm able to enjoy things a little more at this stage. My mom decides to go visit other family members at this time. I tell her to go. I will be ok. While she is away. I believe I can keep things under control.

I'm still on meds at this time. It's me and my two children are home now. My son is very helpful. He fixes me something to eat and brings me my meds. It was the reason for me being able to make it through the day. People would ask my mom how was I doing and she would respond Tyniesha is doing well. For the most part I was ok and mom would call regularly to check on me.

The next week was different it started on Saturday. I noticed I felt weak and couldn't eat. I had a partial headache. I was pretty much under the weather this day. I left my children to go for what they know. Good thing my son was skilled at preparing food. I thank God that my children were with me it made up the difference. He used them to carry me, and was working in the process as well. The next day was Sunday. I felt horrible.

I didn't know what had happened, but there was a change in the way I was feeling. I still manage to talk to God during all of this. My appetite decreased and I felt very dizzy. My spirit however kept saying don't lay in it. Go to church where healing comes from. I listened and followed. I knew it was the voice of God talking to me. I got my spirit of fight. I got dressed and my children too. Although affliction was upon me so was the power of God. He strengthened me enough to get there.

The whole way I felt bad, but he still had me pushing. I made it to service, and just sat there. I didn't have much strength to participate. After service I felt worse than before, and it wasn't letting up. I started crying and my tears was flowing. They were asking me was I ok, and I responded, "I don't feel good." I was going into a state of Lodebar.

It's a state of mind that would cause one to feel alone, and as if no one understands what you go through. On the road home I really started letting the tears flow silently. I was wiping my face with my hands. I was sobbing hysterically. Suddenly a song started playing that said Although I go through sickness and symptoms comes upon my body.

I'm still going to trust God, and give him praise because God hasn't forgotten me. The song touched my spirit, and I immediately knew God was meeting me right where I was. I quickly was reminded of the promises of God. I stopped crying. I still felt bad physically. I got in the house. I made me something to eat. I was able to eat and went to sleep because it was about eleven pm at night. The next day I felt even worse I now noticed sickness was coming upon me.

I called my mom asked her to return home early because I can't do this by myself. She wasn't talking in my favor, and I was trying to figure out where her mind was because she knew my condition. I got off the phone with her and called others. They all became concerned about my status. Maybe her leaving wasn't the best idea or was it?

I called the doctor office because I was also out of meds. They said they would call me back, but no one did. I started back throwing up, and that was really scaring me. I said, "Oh no! I'm going back!" I was lying in bed and started crying again. I was crying to God saying I don't understand I don't know what to do! Help me! please God!

Then a voice quietly said, "Go into Worship." I trusted the voice of God. I listened and followed. I receive strength to put on a Worship song to take me to that place in God in the spirit. I was still laying down, but I lift my hands and began repeating the words to the song. I then began speaking in tongues to communicate with God. I found myself receiving strength to sit up, and close my eyes. I notice all the symptoms I was feeling was disappearing!

God had brought me to a place in him where I felt joy, and no pain at all! I also felt his glory shining on me as I was in his presence. This was all while laying on my sick bed. After this encounter with God. I felt much better, and had strength that I couldn't even explain. I now had God's spirit all around me, and I could feel the difference.

I fell in love with God even more after this because every time Satan had an attack out on me. My God had a plan to rescue me! I Give God all the praise, all the honor, and the glory forever! Amen

God's Glory

✝

The things of God aren't natural to us. We are in a world where darkness, and sorrow is Great. From relationships with others to everything we learn straight from the womb. A baby comes into the world crying because he or she is feeling the pains of the world. We aren't taught that. We are natural to sin, sickness, and also hurt.

Sin and disobedience to God is Great. Gods ways aren't our ways. His thoughts aren't our thoughts. Our minds can't get a grasp of the way God does things. He has hidden himself from us for a reason of protection. He already knows the flesh can't handle seeing him. That's why flesh can't enter into heaven. It wars with the spirit and we can only get to God through the spirit.

We have to be brought into light. Satan has confused the masses with what he considers light, but what he considers light is total darkness to God. We follow after the enemy at first until we come into the full knowledge of God. Everything that we have been taught that goes directly against God. Believing in God is deeper than going to a service every now and then confessing by mouth that we believe.

We have to gain relationship with God. We have to seek God's face, and we have to surrender our whole life to God. That means give up every sin God isn't pleased with. People think because church was boring. They don't want to go or they don't want conviction to fall on them. When we don't know God. Church doesn't even make sense and your just there like a zombie. That is because you don't have a spirit of God. We don't know praise.

We don't acknowledge worship, or understand the gift of tongues. When the spirit of God comes over us then we learn praise, acknowledge worship, and understand gift of tongues. God sent his son that whoever believes, and confess by mouth that he died on the cross shall be saved. It isn't make-believe it is a true story, and you have to have faith to get there. Faith is everything to God, and it's impossible to please him without it.

God isn't going to just come to us. He will however create a situation to get our attention. So, we can come to him. I didn't notice these things until I surrendered to him, and followed what he gave me. I'm glad he pulled me out of my mess and changed my walk, and talk. He loves us forever! The enemy is the only enemy to God's people.

He keeps making us think we are each other's enemy. We aren't! When we see each other as our enemy! We are now seeing God as our enemy! That's why God warns us and then causes his wrath to come upon us. So, to love him is to be like him because he loves us no matter what. It is he who have made us and not we ourselves.

So, when we have a heart of stone that isn't like him. God doesn't hate us! God hates sin. He wants us to have a heart of flesh. Which means continue to show unconditional love as he has done to us. The face of Jesus was also revealed to me in a dream. It's nothing like the pictures we have of him. I never had any idea what he looked like until this vision was revealed to me. And I saw the face of a man in the sky standing tall and big.

He was arrayed in a light that covered him from the crown of his head to the soles of his feet. He was in a huge cloud that appeared in the sky. He was gazing so I know he was alive. He turned his head and his hair was white and long with a light grey streak in the middle. He was looking at everyone on earth, and everyone was looking in amazement. We were shocked when the Son of man was revealed before us and he had come back to reign upon his throne.

His skin wasn't like flesh, but more like armor, and it was dark like the color of tea. He also had Great power and glory that I couldn't explain but felt it very strong like nothing I ever known. He had on a long white plain robe that was all the way to his feet. He had the look of a human but very distinctive. His eyes were glowing, and he didn't have a mustache or beard. A spiritual body in the present. I was so touched by this vision I keep it in my heart waiting for the day that I get to see him face to face. All hail my King! I give God all the praise all the honor and all the Glory! Forever Amen.

Lightning Source UK Ltd.
Milton Keynes UK
UKHW021958230120
357514UK00006B/67